Parenting Interactions with Children: Checklist of Observations Linked to Outcomes (PICCOLO™) User's Guide

Parenting Interactions with Children: Checklist of Observations Linked to Outcomes (PICCOLO™) User's Guide

by

Lori A. Roggman, Ph.D.

Gina A. Cook, Ph.D.

Mark S. Innocenti, Ph.D.

Vonda Jump Norman, Ph.D.

Katie Christiansen, Ph.D.

and

Sheila Anderson, Ph.D.

Utah State University, Logan

·P·A·U·L·H·
BROOKES
PUBLISHING Cº ®

Baltimore • London • Sydney

Paul H. Brookes Publishing Co.
Post Office Box 10624
Baltimore, Maryland 21285-0624

www.brookespublishing.com

PICCOLO™ and the following logo are trademarks of
Paul H. Brookes Publishing Co., Inc.: Ⓟ ⓘ Ⓒ Ⓒ Ⓞ Ⓛ Ⓞ

Typeset by Integrated Publishing Solutions, Inc., Grand Rapids, Michigan.
Manufactured in the United States of America by
Sheridan Books, Inc., Chelsea, Michigan.

Cover photo © istockphoto/lostinbids. Other photos © istockphoto/lisegagne,
© istockphoto/InCommunicado, © istockphoto/andipantz, © istockphoto/nyul.

Library of Congress Cataloging-in-Publication Data

Roggman, Lori A., author.
  Parenting interactions with children: checklist of observations linked to outcomes :
PICCOLO user's guide / by Lori A. Roggman, Ph.D., Gina A. Cook, Ph.D., Mark S.
Innocenti, Ph.D., Vonda Jump Norman, Ph.D., Katie Christiansen, Ph.D., and Sheila
Anderson, Ph.D.
     pages   cm
  Includes bibliographical references and index.
  ISBN-13: 978-1-59857-302-2 (pbk.)
  ISBN-10: 1-59857-302-0 (pbk.)
  1. Home-based family services—United States.   2. Parents—Services for—United States.
I. Title.
  HV699.R655 2013
  362.82'640973—dc23   2013000436

British Library Cataloguing in Publication data are available from the British Library.

2023 2022 2021 2020 2019

10   9   8   7   6   5   4   3

Contents

About the Authors

Lori A. Roggman, Ph.D., Professor in the Department of Family, Consumer, and Human Development, Emma Eccles Jones College of Education and Human Services, Utah State University, Logan, Utah 84322

Dr. Roggman's research focuses on parenting and children's early development. She has extensive experience in home visiting research, integrating theory-based inquiry with program evaluation and application to policy and practice. She is a strong methodologist with expertise in observational data collection and longitudinal analysis and has authored several measures used extensively by researchers and practitioners. Dr. Roggman was the lead author of *Developmental Parenting: A Guide for Early Childhood Practitioners* (with L. Boyce & M. Innocenti; Paul H. Brookes Publishing Co., 2008), and Principal Investigator of a local research team for the national Early Head Start Research and Evaluation Project.

Gina A. Cook, Ph.D., Research Scientist, Center for Persons with Disabilities, and Research Assistant Professor, Department of Family, Consumer, and Human Development, Emma Eccles Jones College of Education and Human Services, Utah State University, Logan, Utah 84322

Dr. Cook's work focuses on longitudinal developmental processes and supportive environments in homes, centers, and preschools related to children's school readiness, especially for groups at risk due to income level or disability. She has worked on the Early Head Start Research and Evaluation Project and has extensive experience as a program evaluator. Dr. Cook has been a Head Start teaching coach and an early intervention home visitor trainer.

Mark S. Innocenti, Ph.D., Director, Research and Evaluation Division, Center for Persons with Disabilities, and Associate Professor, Department of Psychology, Emma Eccles Jones College of Education and Human Services, Utah State University, Logan, Utah 84322

Dr. Innocenti has more than 30 years of experience working with infants and young children at risk and with disabilities and their families in multiple research and model demonstration projects. Using an interdisciplinary model that recognizes the contribution of different disciplines and stakeholders, his research is conducted in and for communities. Recent projects focus on assessment and curriculum, home visiting effectiveness, and preschool intervention to prevent later special education.

Vonda Jump Norman, Ph.D., Senior Research Scientist, Center for Persons with Disabilities, Emma Eccles Jones College of Education and Human Services, Utah State University, Logan, Utah 84322

Dr. Jump Norman's research focuses on promoting optimal development of children experiencing high levels of stress, whether it be due to orphanage environments, poverty, or adverse life events. She is an engaging trainer who focuses on how empirical research applies to real-life situations for staff, teachers, home visitors, and parents. She is a co-investigator on the Cache County, Utah, National Children's Study and actively collaborates with international partners to improve the early development of young children.

Katie Christiansen, Ph.D., PICCOLO™ Researcher and Site Coordinator, Early Head Start Research and Evaluation Project, Department of Family, Consumer, and Human Development, Emma Eccles Jones College of Education and Human Services, Utah State University, Logan, Utah 84322

Dr. Christiansen has worked on several projects as a home visitor trainer. She has extensive experience in child assessment, video observation, preschool evaluation, and teacher evaluation. She is particularly interested in children's language development and reading acquisition. Dr. Christiansen worked as an assessor examining reading scores of Native American children. She used early PICCOLO data to study parenting interactions in a Spanish-speaking population in relation to child development.

Sheila Anderson, Ph.D., Executive Director, Utah Association for the Education of Young Children, Salt Lake City, Utah 84125

Dr. Anderson has more than 20 years of experience in the field of early childhood, as an early childhood classroom teacher and as an instructor and mentor of early childhood professionals. Her work focuses on the effects on child development of early parenting and teacher interactions with children from families of low-income and ethnic minority backgrounds. She received a Head Start Graduate Student Research Scholars grant to test PICCOLO™ as an observational measure of fathers' early parenting behaviors for use by early childhood practitioners.

PICCOLO™ Research Team, Technical Support, Funding, and Program Partners

User's Guide Authors

Lori A. Roggman
Gina A. Cook
Mark S. Innocenti
Vonda Jump Norman
Katie Christiansen
Sheila Anderson

Research Team

Lori A. Roggman
Mark S. Innocenti
Gina A. Cook
Vonda Jump Norman
Katie Christiansen
Sheila Anderson
James Akers
Cora Price
LauraMichele Gardner
Nicole Todd
Krista Gurko

Technical Support

Tyler Monson
Todd Newman

Emma Eccles Jones College of Education and Human Resources
Utah State University
Developed as a Head Start University Partnership
funded by DHHS/ACYF Grant # 90YF0050
with support from a Community/University Research
Initiative grant at Utah State University

Program Partners

Bear River Head Start, Logan, Utah—Sarah Thurgood, Director
Head Start Parent Child Centers, Layton, Utah—Kathy Shaw Sartor, Director
Guadalupe Schools Early Childhood Program, Salt Lake City, Utah—
Patty Walker, Director

Acknowledgments

Parenting Interactions with Children: Checklist of Observations Linked to Outcomes (PICCOLO™) development was supported by the Administration for Children Youth and Families (ACF) Grant #90YF0050 and a Community/University Research Initiative grant at Utah State University.

We are grateful to the practitioners in our program partners and to the many student observers who helped develop the PICCOLO measure. We are especially grateful to the parents and children in the video clips used to develop PICCOLO. Thousands of parents and children in the video clips have provided a rich opportunity for us to learn more about parenting. Most of the parenting and child video clips and outcome data used for developing PICCOLO were from the Early Head Start Research and Evaluation Project, conducted in collaboration with the Administration for Youth and Families, Mathematica Policy Research, and local research partners at 17 sites. We are grateful to the Early Head Start Research Consortium and the Head Start Bureau for archiving those video clips so they would be available for further research.

Research institutions in the Early Head Start Research Consortium (and principal researchers) include ACF (Rachel Chazan Cohen, Judith Jerald, Esther Kresh, Helen Raikes, Louisa Tarullo); Catholic University of America (Michaela Farber, Lynn Milgram Mayer, Harriet Liebow, Christine Sabatino, Nancy Taylor, Elizabeth Timberlake, Shavaun Wall); Columbia University (Lisa Berlin, Christy Brady-Smith, Jeanne Brooks-Gunn, Alison Sidle Fuligni); Harvard University (Catherine Ayoub, Barbara Alexander Pan, Catherine Snow); Iowa State University (Dee Draper, Gayle Luze, Susan McBride, Carla Peterson); Mathematica Policy Research (Kimberly Boller, Ellen Eliason Kisker, John M. Love, Diane Paulsell, Christine Ross, Peter Schochet, Cheri Vogel, Welmoet van Kammen); Medical University of South Carolina (Richard Faldowski, Gui-Young Hong, Susan Pickrel); Michigan State University (Hiram Fitzgerald, Tom Reischl, Rachel Schiffman); New York University (Mark Spellmann, Catherine Tamis-LeMonda); University of Arkansas (Robert Bradley, Mark Swanson, Leanne Whiteside-Mansell); University of California, Los Angeles (Carollee Howes, Claire Hamilton); University of Colorado Health Sciences Center (Robert Emde, Jon Korfmacher, JoAnn Robinson, Paul Spicer, Norman Watt); University of Kansas (Jane Atwater, Judith Carta, Jean Ann Summers); University of Missouri–Columbia (Mark Fine, Jean Ispa, Kathy Thornburg); University of Pittsburgh (Carol McAllister, Beth Green, Robert McCall); University of Washington School of Education (Eduardo Armijo, Joseph Stowitschek); University of Washington School of Nursing (Kathryn Barnard, Susan Spieker); and Utah State University (USU; Lisa Boyce, Catherine Callow-Heusser, Gina A. Cook, Lori A. Roggman).

Additional extant observations and data were from studies conducted by members of the PICCOLO research team at USU in the Department of Family, Consumer, and Human Development and at the Early Intervention Research Institute.

To all of the dedicated people
who work with families to promote
developmentally supportive parenting
of infants and young children
so the next generation
can succeed in our world

1

Understanding PICCOLO™

Parenting Interactions with Children: Checklist of Observations Linked to Outcomes (PICCOLO™) is a checklist of 29 observable, developmentally supportive parenting behaviors with children ages 10–47 months in four domains—Affection, Responsiveness, Encouragement, and Teaching. PICCOLO is reliable, valid, easy to learn, and practical to use. It has been tested on a large ethnically diverse sample and is available in multiple languages.

PICCOLO is useful for programs for infants, toddlers, and young children that emphasize positive parenting interactions as a way to promote children's early development. To guide interventions and ensure program effectiveness, practitioners need a valid measure of parenting interactions with established links to child outcomes.

PICCOLO is research based and was tested by using longitudinal data and video observations from the Early Head Start Research and Evaluation Project archive along with video observations and data from other research studies by the authors. PICCOLO helps programs see progress in parenting outcomes, but more important, PICCOLO helps practitioners observe a wide range of parenting behaviors so they can provide positive feedback and help parents do more of the positive things they already know how to do and think are important to do.

WHAT KIND OF PARENTING INTERACTIONS DOES PICCOLO™ MEASURE?

PICCOLO is a strengths-based measure of parenting interactions that predicts children's early social, cognitive, and language development. Social development includes the development of attachment security, self-regulation, and positive social-interaction behaviors. Cognitive development includes exploration, problem solving, and reasoning. Language development includes communication, vocabulary, and emergent literacy. These are broad, important areas of early child development that provide a foundation for school and life success.

In our work, the parenting behaviors that help children develop over time are referred to as *developmental parenting* (Roggman, Boyce, & Innocenti, 2008). Developmental parenting behaviors develop and change over time and are the parenting behaviors that parenting support programs, such as Early Head Start or Parents as Teachers, typically aim to help parents develop or increase. PICCOLO was designed for programs such as these to help parents increase the behaviors that sup-

1

port children's early development. Four domains of developmental parenting are measured by PICCOLO:

- *Affection:* Warmth, physical closeness, and positive expressions toward child

- *Responsiveness:* Responding to child's cues, emotions, words, interests, and behaviors

- *Encouragement:* Active support of exploration, effort, skills, initiative, curiosity, creativity, and play

- *Teaching:* Shared conversation and play, cognitive stimulation, explanations, and questions

Because each individual parent may have strengths in different domains, it is important to measure all four domains. For a summary of the research literature supporting these domains, see Table 1.1. All of these parenting domains are important for children's early development, so several specific parent behaviors may predict a single child outcome. Also, positive parenting interactions can support children's development in multiple areas, so a single parenting behavior may predict several child outcomes.

Parenting strengths—what the parent already believes is important to do and is comfortable doing with his or her child—are a valuable resource for increasing the developmental support available to young children. By using an observational measure of a diverse set of developmental parenting behaviors, home visitors and other early childhood practitioners can identify behaviors parents can readily increase to provide more support for their children's early development.

If developmentally supportive parenting is a program goal, it should be assessed in order to guide program activities and measured as a program outcome to ensure program quality over time. PICCOLO is an observation measure that shows what parents can do to support their children's development.

WHY USE PICCOLO™?

PICCOLO identifies parenting behaviors that support early child development. Items describing specific developmentally supportive parenting behaviors were carefully worded, tested, and selected. Each item was identified in the research literature as a predictor of positive child outcomes and then shown in our research to predict positive child outcomes in a low-income multi-ethnic sample.

PICCOLO shows what parents are comfortable doing with their children and what they think is important to do. Because the measure is based on an observation of parent–child interaction, it shows what parents are comfortable doing in the presence of other people and believe are good ways to interact with their children. Although observational measures can be criticized for making people "pretend" to be better than they are, this is also the strength of observational measures. Young children are unlikely to be able to pretend to behave as better children than they are, but their parents want to be seen in the best light—so parents' observed behaviors are likely to reflect what they think will show them to be good parents. They are unlikely, however, to do things that they do not know how to do or are uncomfortable doing with their child.

PICCOLO can help early childhood practitioners provide feedback about positive parenting. By observing and commenting on the positive parenting behaviors

Table 1.1. Summary of research literature evidence for the Parenting Interactions with Children: Checklist of Observations Linked to Outcomes (PICCOLO™) domains

PICCOLO domain	Evidence of outcomes	References
Affection	Warmth, including affection and positive affect, is related to less antisocial behavior, better adjustment, more compliance, greater cognitive ability, and better school readiness.	Caspi et al. (2004); Dodici, Draper, and Peterson (2003); Estrada, Arsenio, Hess, and Holloway (1987); Farah et al. (2008); Kim-Cohen, Moffitt, Caspi, and Taylor (2004); MacDonald (1992); Petrill and Deater-Deckard (2004); Sroufe, Egeland, and Kreutzer (1990)
Responsiveness	Responding sensitively to infant cues, expressions of needs or interests, and efforts at communication is related to more secure attachment, better cognitive development, better social development and adjustment, better language development, fewer behavior problems, better emotional regulation, and more empathy.	Bernier, Carlson, and Whipple (2010); Booth, Rose-Krasnor, McKinnon, and Rubin (1994); Brotman et al. (2009); Davidov and Grusec (2006); Hart, Nelson, Robinson, Olsen, and McNeilly-Choque (1998); Hirsh-Pasek and Burchinal (2006); Landry, Swank, Assel, Smith, and Vellet (2001); Spencer and Meadow-Orlans (1996); Tamis-LeMonda, Bornstein, and Baumwell (2001); Volker, Keller, Lohaus, Cappenberg, and Chasiotis (1999); Wakschlag and Hans (1999)
Encouragement	Encouraging children's interests and self-direction and not being too restrictive or intrusive is related to greater independence and security, less negativity, more willingness to try challenging tasks, better cognitive and social development, and better language development.	Bernier et al. (2010); Frodi, Bridges, and Grolnick (1985); Hart and Risley (1995); Ispa et al. (2004); Kelley, Brownell, and Campbell (2000); Kelly, Morisset, Barnard, Hammond, and Booth (1996); Landry, Smith, Miller-Loncar, and Swank (1997); Meins, Fernyhough, Fradley, and Tuckey (2001)
Teaching	Talking with children, responding to their communications, and playing together is related to better cognitive and social development, better language development, and better emergent literacy skills.	Bingham (2007); Brotman et al. (2009); Farah et al. (2008); Hart and Risley (1995); Hockenberger, Goldstein, and Haas (1999); Kim-Cohen et al. (2004); Laakso, Poikkeus, Eklund, and Lyytinen (1999); Tamis-LeMonda et al. (2001)

that are observed, practitioners can point out to parents what they are already able to do to support their children's development.

PICCOLO can be used to do the following:

- Assess positive parenting behaviors that predict good child outcomes
- Guide individualized positive parenting interventions with families
- Track positive parenting outcomes of a parenting support program

PICCOLO was developed as a tool for practitioners. It was designed to have characteristics that programs asked for in a parenting measure. PICCOLO is positive, practical, versatile, culturally sensitive, valid, and reliable. With funding from the Administration for Children, Youth, and Families (ACYF) and additional support from Utah State University, the PICCOLO development team

- Reviewed studies linking parenting interaction behaviors with child outcomes
- Used the video and data archives of the Early Head Start Research and Evaluation Project

- Collected new data from more than 4,500 video observations of more than 2,000 families

- Observed parenting behaviors in these videos with children ages 10–47 months

- Evaluated items describing parent behavior based on reliability and validity

- Selected the 29 best items from more than 100 items

- Provided observation guidelines for each item

- Tested the measure in infant-toddler programs

  PICCOLO is practical because it is

- *Research based:* It assesses parenting behaviors linked to child outcomes in research.

- *Culturally relevant*: Items are based on observations of three major ethnic groups: European Americans, Latino Americans, and African Americans. All items predict similar child outcomes regardless of ethnic group. All items were reliably coded by observers from the same ethnic group as the observed family and by observers from different ethnic groups.

- *Useful*: PICCOLO helps practitioners assess positive parenting strengths, plan activities, track outcomes, and identify parenting strengths to encourage.

- *Easy to learn and use:* Practitioners learn to use PICCOLO reliably in 8–12 hours. PICCOLO can be scored from a 10-minute observation, live or from video.

- *Outcomes oriented*: PICCOLO can be used to monitor parent outcomes and program effectiveness.

WHAT DO PRACTITIONERS SAY ABOUT PICCOLO™?

Practitioners who have used PICCOLO say that it helps them be better observers:

> *"I saw things I didn't see before—how little the mom actually speaks to her child."*
>
> *"PICCOLO helped me observe more concretely...instead of just having a feeling."*
>
> *"I really thought that I would not observe as much as I did."*

Practitioners find PICCOLO helpful for identifying what parents already do with their children:

> *"PICCOLO helps highlight weak and strong skills."*

Practitioners use PICCOLO to guide planning for home visits:

> *"You see things you might want to work on with the parent in the next visit...things you don't always see."*

Practitioners also find they can use PICCOLO directly with the parents:

> *"PICCOLO is useful for parents to do so they can look at their skills."*
>
> *"Viewing the video with the family while identifying examples of the positive behaviors was very empowering to the parents."*
>
> *"While discussing the PICCOLO assessment with the parent and commenting on parenting strengths, the parent seemed excited about those strengths and a bit relieved to be doing many things 'right.'"*

Practitioners say that PICCOLO helps them encourage developmental parenting:

> *"PICCOLO is a good tool to help parents understand their importance."*
>
> *"It was neat to see the parent's reaction as I listed off the small things she did during the PICCOLO that can mean a lot for her son's development."*
>
> *"When parents know what they are doing well, it is likely they will do more of it."*

Practitioners use PICCOLO to plan their activities with families:

> *"PICCOLO makes it easier to develop lesson plans for home visits."*

Practitioners found PICCOLO to be easy to use:

> *"PICCOLO was easy to learn and really user friendly!"*
>
> *"I was completely amazed how quickly I was picking up on many behaviors."*

Overall, practitioners were positive about PICCOLO:

> *"It works for me and my families."*
>
> *"It's cutting edge for the birth to 3 group."*
>
> *"It works in my community."*

PICCOLO™ PSYCHOMETRIC PROPERTIES

Our tests of PICCOLO demonstrated strong psychometric properties.

Interrater Reliability

Interrater reliability shows that different observers score PICCOLO the same way. Reliability was estimated from correlations between pairs of observers for each domain score. Absolute agreement was estimated by counting, for each item, the percent of cases on which observers agreed on the score, averaging across all items within each domain and then averaging across domains.

- Reliability between pairs of observers averaged .77 across domain scores.

- Absolute item agreement between raters averaged 75% across domains.

Scale Reliability

Scale reliability was assessed by conducting a factor analysis and by estimating coefficient alpha. A single factor structure was tested within each domain to ensure that factor loadings for each item were greater than an acceptable minimum of .40. Coefficient alpha was examined for each domain to ensure that it exceeded the acceptable minimum of .65.

- Single factor structure was supported in each domain, with average factor loading .65.

- Internal consistency *alpha* across the four domains averaged .78.

Content Validity

Practitioners who work with parents and young children rated PICCOLO behaviors as *important* or *very important,* averaging 2.58 on a 0- to 3-point scale. As another indication of content validity, parents whose children were enrolled in Early Head Start for at least 1 year showed significantly higher Responsiveness, Encouragement, and Teaching scores than parents in the comparison group. PICCOLO thus measures parenting behaviors that experts believe are important and that programs such as Early Head Start can increase.

Construct Validity

Concurrent correlations for PICCOLO domains and total scores were statistically significant when tested in relation to other measures of the same observations of parenting interactions (Brady-Smith, Fauth, & Brooks-Gunn, 2005), including overall PICCOLO with overall supportiveness over time, $r = .62$, and each specific domain with the most similar parenting construct:

- Affection with positive regard, $r = .61$

- Responsiveness with sensitivity, $r = .46$

- Encouragement with overall supportiveness, $r = .52$, and negatively with intrusiveness, $r = -.35$

- Teaching with cognitive stimulation, $r = .59$

Predictive Validity

PICCOLO scores at ages 1, 2, and 3 years significantly predicted children's cognitive-language development at age 3, $r = .21-.27$, and at age 5, $r = .24-.27$, and significantly predicted overall development, including cognitive-language and social development at age 3, $r = .19-.24$, and at age 5, $r = .23-.25$.

Specific PICCOLO domain scores also predicted child cognitive, language, and social-emotional outcomes at ages 3 and 5. Both the individual items and the total domain scores at ages 1, 2, and 3 were examined in relation to child outcomes at later ages. Predictive correlations for PICCOLO total and domain scores were statistically significant for the following outcomes from the children's developmental assessments:

- *Cognitive outcomes,* as measured by the Bayley Scales of Infant Development Mental Development Index (Bayley, 1993) at age 3 and the Woodcock-Johnson Applied Problems subscale (Woodcock & Johnson, 1989) at age 5

- *Language and emergent literacy outcomes,* as measured by the Peabody Picture Vocabulary Test–III (Dunn & Dunn, 1997) of receptive vocabulary at ages 3 and 5 and the Woodcock-Johnson Letter-Word subscale (Woodcock & Johnson, 1989) at age 5

- *Social-emotional outcomes* as measured by the Bayley Scales of Infant Development Behavior Rating Scale of emotion regulation (Bayley, 1993) at age 3 and the Child Behavior Checklist aggression subscale (Achenbach & Rescorla, 2000) at ages 3 and 5

Note: Additional details are available in the Technical Report (Appendix A) about the methodology used to develop PICCOLO and statistical data used to evaluate the psychometric strengths of the measure.

WHY USE A MEASURE OF POSITIVE PARENTING INTERACTIONS?

Practitioners who use PICCOLO include home visitors, child development specialists, family educators, parenting class leaders, infant mental health clinicians, or people in other similar positions who work with parents to support their children's development. Programs aiming to promote positive parenting use PICCOLO. Programs using intervention strategies that build on family strengths find PICCOLO especially useful. Practitioners who use a strengths-based approach appreciate the emphasis on positive parenting in the PICCOLO measure.

A strengths-based approach to working with parents of infants and young children builds on parents' strengths to support the child's development. This approach to working with families includes identifying and then using the family's strengths (Green, McAllister, & Tarte, 2005). The strategy of focusing on parents' available skills and resources can also be referred to as a *mutual competence* approach and has support in theory, research, and practice (e.g., Barnard, Morisset, & Spieker, 1993; Bernstein, Campbell, & Akers, 2001; Bernstein, Hans, & Percansky, 1991; Goldberg, 1977). This approach requires careful observation of parents' capacities to support their children's early development.

Practitioners who work directly with parents in infant-toddler and early childhood programs often take a strengths-based approach when they focus on what families are already doing well or already have as resources. They use these strengths as a foundation for building further strengths and addressing challenges that may be facing a particular family in supporting their children's development. These programs and practitioners need a tool to monitor progress as parents build their skills for supporting children's early development. PICCOLO is a tool that can be used to assess strengths, reveal needs, and monitor change.

Parents show strengths in various ways: by showing affection, by being responsive, by encouraging their children to try new things, and by teaching their children. PICCOLO helps practitioners identify how each parent shows his or her strengths. PICCOLO lists multiple observable behavioral indicators of important dimensions of positive parenting interactions to assist practitioners in identifying family strengths.

The kinds of positive interactions parents already enjoy with their children provide an opportunity for increasing the frequency of such interactions, particularly those interactions that are known to support children's development in social, language, and cognitive domains (e.g., Culp, Hubbs-Tait, Culp, & Starost, 2000; Estrada, Arsenio, Hess, & Holloway, 1987; Fewell & Deutscher, 2002; Gardner, Ward, Burton, & Wilson, 2003; Hubbs-Tait, Culp, Culp, & Miller, 2002; Lee, Murry, Brody, & Parker, 2002).

Observing positive parenting interactions, however, can be challenging for practitioners who do not always know what specific behaviors to observe. Depending on their education, training, and experiences, practitioners may notice some types of parenting behaviors more than others and may not always notice some parenting behaviors that are important for children's development. PICCOLO guides practitioner observations by providing specific behaviors for practitioners to observe and a detailed description of each behavior. Chapter 2 provides information about learning to use PICCOLO.

2

Learning to Use PICCOLO™

The following steps are one way for practitioners to become familiar with PICCOLO and get comfortable using it in their work with families. Practitioners may need to adapt these steps to their individual needs.

Step 1.   Read through the PICCOLO items and the coding guidelines that are provided for each item (PICCOLO is available in Spanish in Appendix B and currently is being translated into French, German, and Turkish). The PICCOLO measure shows detailed coding guidelines. These guidelines provide detailed definitions of every parenting behavior item. Additional observational notes are provided in this chapter.

Step 2.   Read through this user's guide to get basic information about PICCOLO. Some information is also available on *The PICCOLO™ Training DVD: Implementation and Scoring* (Roggman, Cook, Innocenti, & Jump Norman, 2013). This user's guide also includes a summary of the psychometric data on PICCOLO and suggestions for using PICCOLO with families.

Step 3.   Watch video clips of parent–child interactions on *The PICCOLO™ Training DVD*. First, watch the 1-minute clips for each domain: Affection, Responsiveness, Encouragement, and Teaching. The example videos, which are 5-minute and 10-minute video clips, offer an opportunity for scoring PICCOLO behaviors and comparing your scores to our scores for those clips, which are provided in Appendix C.

Step 4.   Practice observing families you know. Video-record a parent and child playing together. Practice scoring the video by watching it with someone else. Score the PICCOLO domains separately and then compare your ratings. Watch the video again and discuss the differences in your ratings until you can come to an agreement for all items. Repeat with another video clip, and continue this process until you initially disagree by only 1 point on 3 or fewer items per domain.

WHAT ELSE DO I NEED TO KNOW TO USE PICCOLO™ ACCURATELY?

We have trained many people to use PICCOLO accurately and have answered many questions about PICCOLO. We answer some general questions in Chapter 4.

When questions have been raised about specific parenting behaviors in relation to PICCOLO scoring, we have kept notes about each of the items that provide helpful clarification. Table 2.1 shows these notes with each item and guideline.

Table 2.1. Observation notes for the four domains

Item	Guideline	Additional observation notes
Affection		
1. Speaks in a warm tone of voice	Parent's voice is positive in tone and may show enthusiasm or tenderness. A parent who speaks little but very warmly should be coded highly.	Flat and toneless or sarcastic and demanding voices are not warm. Score as 0 unless there were some moments of warmth. Warmth may sound like *motherese* (e.g., exaggerated intonation, high pitch), though not always. Enjoyment and interest may also sound warm. The parent's voice cannot be harsh and warm at the same time. Sometimes a parent is warm at the beginning but the warmth fades, so the last part of the observation is important to consider. For a score of 2, the parent's voice should be mostly warm throughout.
2. Smiles at child	Parent directs smiles toward child, but parent and child do not need to be looking at each other when smile occurs. Includes small smiles.	For a score of 2, the parent should smile about once per minute and needs to be looking at or clearly facing the child. Smiling should be about the child. Ignore smiles to the camera or to another child or adult or smiling about something funny in a book or toy. Also ignore smiles that seem to be from nervous laughter or self-consciousness. The child does NOT have to be looking at the parent.
3. Praises child	Parent says something positive about child characteristics or about what child is doing. A "thank you" can be coded as praise.	Praise is always in a positive tone, in response to child behavior, and *after* rather than *during* the child's behavior. Praise is typically in response to the child's accomplishment or compliance. It includes "yeah" and "all right" if the words are a clear, positive response to something the child has done. Consider cultural context and slang (e.g., "sweet," "cool"). Sometimes praise can also be coded as "positive expressions" or "shows emotional support" but not always, so consider guidelines carefully. Consider missed opportunities: The parent frequently asks the child to do something but never or rarely praises the child when he or she complies.
4. Is physically close to child	Parent is within easy arm's reach of child, comfortably able to soothe or help. Consider context: Expect more closeness for book reading than for playing house.	The parent should be close enough to the child to easily soothe, show affection, or give or get help or reassurance. The parent should be no more than an arm's length away. The parent should not be avoiding physical proximity or contact. Look at the parent's body posture: leaning toward the child, showing physical affection, or repositioning to remain close.
5. Uses positive expressions with child	Parent says positive things or uses words like "honey," "kiddo," or an affectionate nickname. (*Note:* Emphasis on verbal expressions.)	Consider other terms such as "son," "buddy," and "mijo." Consider the cultural and language context (e.g., diminutives in Spanish). Other positive expressions include "I love you," "You are so silly," "You are my baboo," and "Are you my little girl?" Compliments that are not praise for specific behaviors (e.g., "You are pretty like your mommy") can also be considered positive expressions. A shortened form of a name (e.g., "Ty" for Tyler) may be used as a positive expression but is weaker than a more affectionate nickname. Terms that are more strongly positive or affectionate carry more weight for scoring this item.

Item	Guideline	Additional observation notes
6. Is engaged in interacting with child	Parent is actively involved together *with* child, not just with activities or with another adult.	This item is not scoring *parallel play*, when parent and child are each playing but doing their own thing next to each other. The parent and child need to be playing together and focused on the same activity with the parent being neither directive nor passive. For younger children, the parent is typically engaging with the same toy as the child, but with more verbal children, the parent may just be talking about the toy or the child's behavior. For a score of 2, the parent is involved most of the time.
7. Shows emotional warmth	Parent shows enjoyment, fondness, or other positive emotion about child and directed to child. (*Note*: Includes verbal but emphasis on nonverbal.)	Consider the overall feeling—the parent is having a good time with the child, is positive and interested throughout, and is not bored or wondering how much longer he or she has to play with the child. Physical affection shows warmth. Consider the parent's interest along with warmth, but if the parent is showing some interest but his or her overall emotion is flat, score as 0 unless positive interest is truly directed toward the child and the child is clearly aware of the interest.

Responsiveness

Item	Guideline	Additional observation notes
1. Pays attention to what child is doing	Parent looks at and reacts to what child is doing by making comments, showing interest, helping, *or* otherwise attending to child's actions.	The parent is paying enough attention that the parent could (if asked) describe what the child is doing during most of the observation. Consider missed opportunities: The child tries to show the parent something or calls to the parent and the parent does not look, make comments, or show much interest. Parent engagement in the activity is not required for this item if the parent watches and reacts.
2. Changes pace or activity to meet child's interests or needs	Parent tries a new activity or speeds up or slows down an activity in response to where child looks, what child reaches for, what child says, or emotions child shows.	The parent initiates the change to keep the child engaged in response to the child's getting bored or frustrated. For example, the child is bored with hearing the story so the parent starts asking questions or the child is trying to do something difficult so the parent slows down and gives hints. If the child never loses interest or never tries something difficult, or the parent does not change the pace, score as 0. If the parent never adapts to the child's pace—moves too quickly to a new activity or sticks with an activity too long—score as 0. If the child loses interest right away after the parent has changed the pace or activity, score as 1. The parent can also be scored for changing pace if he or she suggests a new activity but the child does not want to do it and the parent sticks with what the child is already doing.
3. Is flexible about child's change of activities or interests	Parent accepts a child's choice of a new activity or toy *or* shows agreeableness about the change or about child playing in unusual ways with or without toys.	The parent supports the child's initiation. For example, the parent lets the child choose how or when to turn the pages in a book, lets the child explore toys, and is neither directive nor passive. If the child does not initiate anything, score as 0. If the parent is passive or uninvolved, score as 0 because he or she is not being flexible—the parent has to change something he or she is doing, not just go from nothing to nothing.

(continued)

Table 2.1.   *(continued)*

Item	Guideline	Additional observation notes
Responsiveness (continued)		
4. Follows what child is trying to do	Parent both responds to *and* gets involved with child's activities.	This item involves yielding to the child's interests and motivation and doing what the child seems to want or attending to what the child seems interested in. It includes behaviors like repeating what the child says and imitating what the child does, engaging as a play partner in play the child initiates, and helping the child do something if the child is struggling. It involves more than just talking about the toys. If the child does nothing, the parent cannot follow, so score this item as 0. If the child makes only a few initiations but the parent follows each one and gets involved, score as 2.
5. Responds to child's emotions	Parent reacts to child's positive or negative feelings by showing understanding or acceptance, suggesting a solution, reengaging the child, labeling or describing the feeling, showing a similar feeling, or providing sympathy for negative feelings.	For a score of 2, the parent frequently matches the child's expression and intensity of feeling and is neither flat nor harsh. This might be subtle, but a child is always displaying an emotion, even if it is not strong or animated. If a child is disengaged, that is an emotion, and the parent's appropriate response would be to reengage the child in some way or to provide an opportunity for quieter play or rest. The parent may describe emotions by saying what the child likes: "You really like play-ing with cars, don't you?" "You don't like the sound that makes, do you?" or "It feels good, huh?" Consider missed opportunities; for example, if the child is excited about a toy but the parent's emotional expression remains flat.
6. Looks at child when child talks or makes sounds	When child makes sounds, parent clearly looks at child's face or (if eyes or child's face are not visible) parent's position and head movement face toward child.	Other than reading in the lap, the parent generally looks at the child when the child talks. The parent may turn toward the child or simply flash eyes toward the child most of the time when the child vocalizes or speaks. If the parent is already looking in the direction of the child when the child begins to vocalize, then the parent is looking at the child when the child talks or makes sounds. If parent and child are both looking at the same object and talking about it or the parent orients toward the object the child is talking about, that is joint attention and a good parenting behavior, but it does not fit this item. Consider missed opportunities: The child calls to the parent or makes sounds, and the parent does not look toward the child.
7. Replies to child's words or sounds	Parent repeats what child says or sounds child makes, talks about what child says or could be saying, *or* answers child's questions.	For a score of 2, the parent responds to most of the child's vocal sounds. If the child makes no sounds, score as 0. If the child makes only one or two sounds but the parent is consistently responsive, score as 2. Some replies, such as "uh huh" may seem unresponsive; if so, score lower. Consistency is more important than frequency. Consider missed opportunities: The child is talking or making sounds, and the parent says nothing or says very little.

Item	Guideline	Additional observation notes
Encouragement		
1. Waits for child's response after making a suggestion	Parent pauses after saying something the child could do *and* waits for child to answer or do something, whether child actually responds or not.	The parent makes a suggestion for the child to do something specific and then pauses and does not do the activity or action suggested, move the child's hands, or do anything further to interfere with what the child is doing—the opposite of intrusive play. Waiting often looks like the parent is leaning back, has dropped hands, is relaxing, and has an expression of openness and patience. The parent may repeat the suggestion after a few seconds but the tone does not feel impatient or demanding. Suggestions may be phrased as questions such as "Do you want to play with the ball?" or "How about we put the blocks in the basket?" The parent may begin the behavior but then pause to wait for the child's response. This item does not include questions that ask for information such as "What's that?"
2. Encourages child to handle toys	Parent offers toys or says positive things when child shows obvious interest in toys. (Does not include preventing children from mouthing toys.)	This item includes handing toys to the child, showing toys to the child, moving toys closer to the child, demonstrating something with the toy, highlighting toys by moving or using them, making noise with a toy to attract attention, or praising what the child does with the toys. This item could also include imitating what the child does with a toy without interfering or interrupting what the child is doing. The object does not have to be a toy. This item does not include passively watching.
3. Supports child in making choices	Parent allows child to choose activity or toy *and* gets involved with activity or toy child chooses.	The parent can accept the child's choices and get involved or can offer choices and get involved. The parent can offer genuine choices verbally such as by asking, "Which one do you want?" or by describing choices or offering alternative suggestions that are true options. Rhetorical questions such as "Do you want me to read the book?" while opening the book and starting to read do not offer a choice. The parent can offer choices nonverbally by putting more than one toy in reach.
4. Supports child in doing things on his or her own	Parent shows enthusiasm for things child tries to do without help, lets child choose how things are done, *and* lets child try to do things before offering help or suggestions. Parent can be engaged in activities child does "on his or her own."	To get a score of 2, the child must try to do something on his or her own *and* the parent should clearly do at least two of the following three things: 1) show enthusiasm, 2) let the child choose, and 3) let the child try without help. However, even if the parent does not offer help or does not make a suggestion, the parent should still be watching, waiting, and showing interest and positive response to what the child does on his or her own, without interfering, in order to get a score of 2. If the parent does any one of these things—shows enthusiasm or lets the child choose or lets the child try without help, score as 1. If the parent also interferes with the child doing things on his or her own by criticizing or not letting the child have choices, or not letting the child try to do things before offering help or suggestions, do not score as more than a 1. If the child does not try to do anything on his or her own, score as 0.

(continued)

Table 2.1.   *(continued)*

Item	Guideline	Additional observation notes
Encouragement (continued)		
5. Verbally encourages child's efforts	Parent shows verbal enthusiasm, offers positive comments, *or* makes suggestions about child's activity.	This item includes the parent cheering the child on as the child tries to do something. Examples include the following: "Go ahead," "You can do it," "Try again," "You are really working hard," "Go for it," "You can do it," "You're getting it," "Keep trying," and "Try it [slower, faster, softer, harder]." Responses could include describing what the child is doing such as "You are putting all the blocks in the box" or "You are stacking the blocks carefully." This item also includes praise that is for effort: "There you go" or "You did it." This behavior is most likely when the activity is challenging for the child. Consider missed opportunities: The child is trying hard, but the parent does not encourage before, during, or after the event.
6. Offers suggestions to help child	Parent gives hints or makes comments to make things *easier* for child, without interfering with child's play.	The suggestions have to be helpful—something that will make it easier for the child to do what the child seems to be trying to do. Examples include "It's upside down," "Push harder," and "Turn it over." This item also includes hints, such as after asking the child, "What's that?" the parent may say, "Remember, we saw one at Grandma's house last night?" Or if the child is counting or saying the alphabet and gets stuck, the parent may give a hint by saying the next number or letter. Consider missed opportunities: The child is struggling, but the parent offers no suggestions.
7. Shows enthusiasm about what child is doing	Parent makes positive statements, claps hands, or shows other clear positive response to what child is *doing*, including quiet enthusiasm such as patting child, nodding, smiling, or asking child questions about activities.	The enthusiasm needs to be about the child's behavior, not for the toys or the parent's own ideas. Notice quiet parents' enthusiasm shown by nods, interest, and questions. Consider missed opportunities: The parent does not seem enthusiastic or interested when the child is excited about the activity.
Teaching		
1. Explains reasons for something to child	Parent says something that could answer a "why" question, whether child asks a question or not.	The parent's reasons generally have a causal structure and explain how things happen or why they happen, or what happens to something. Some parents use the words "so" or "because" or "if...then." Examples include "Put the lid on so it won't spill," "It can spill if the lid isn't tight because it can come out through the gap between the bottle and the lid," "We have to cook the food so we can eat it," or "If you don't cook the food, then it will make us sick." Explaining how things happen can be a description of a process such as "The snow is on the ground in the winter, but when spring comes it starts to warm up and melt into water for the flowers." This is a less frequent behavior, so one extended or complex explanation can be scored as a 2.

Item	Guideline	Additional observation notes
2. Suggests activities to extend what child is doing	Parent says something child could do to add to what child is already doing but does not interrupt child's interests, actions, or play.	Suggestions must build on what the child is already doing by stating what the child can do to add to how the child is already playing, expand on the play, or make the play more complex. Suggestions to extend play must both build on what the child is doing and add to it in some way.
3. Repeats or expands child's words or sounds	Parent says the same words or makes the same sounds child makes *or* repeats what child says while adding something that adds to the idea.	The parent repeats the child's exact words or repeats the child's sounds, or expands by adding words or sounds to what the child says. If the child says, "Doggie," the parent may say, "That's right; it's a doggie." Or expand with more complexity, such as saying, "Yeah, it's a big brown doggie sitting by his dog house."
4. Labels objects or actions for child	Parent names what child is doing, playing with, or looking at.	Nouns and verbs are labels for objects and actions: "It's a stove, and you can cook with it." When the parent says things like, "The book has a hole," the parent is labeling both the book and the hole. Labels often occur naturally as part of conversation and can be easy to miss. The parent points to pictures in the book: "See here, she is spinning the web," labeling both action (*spinning*) and object (*web*); "That's a stethoscope," labeling an object (*stethoscope*); "You're giving more medicine to the bear," labeling both action (*giving*) and objects (*medicine, bear*). Consider diversity of materials and actions available to label.
5. Engages in pretend play with child	Parent plays make believe in any way—for example, by "eating" pretend food.	Pretending can occur by taking on a role (fighting in rough and tumble play, being the patient in doctor play), using an object to represent something else (pretending a block is a car by moving it on the floor and making car sounds), pretending something is real (eating the pizza, saying the food is hot, making animal sounds for little plastic animals, making car sounds for cars, or making dolls talk), or pretending to be the characters in a book (animating voice and facial expression while reading). The parent actually needs to be pretending, such as by making a statement "as if" the pretending is real, not just narrating the child's pretending. For example, not just saying, "You can pretend to make supper," but "Please make me supper." Not just, "Put the groceries in the cart," but "What else do we need to buy?" It is not enough for parent to describe the child's pretending; the parent must be pretending too in some way.
6. Does activities in a sequence of steps	Parent demonstrates or describes the order of steps or does an activity in a way that a definite order of steps is clear even if parent does not say exactly what the steps are. Book reading counts *only* if parent makes the steps explicit by exaggerating or explaining the steps of reading.	Steps need to occur close together with clear linkages and not be broken up with other activities in between. The step-by-step sequence should be something you could describe easily in words: "First, the child gives the parent the thing to buy. Then, the parent scans it. Then, the child gives her the next thing, and she scans it. They do that for each thing, and then she tells him how much he owes." A sequence of steps often gets repeated, described in words, or explicitly demonstrated in steps. If there is no description or repetition, the demonstration should be of something that could not be done in another sequence (e.g., take the lid off the pot, put

(continued)

Table 2.1.   *(continued)*

Item	Guideline	Additional observation notes
Teaching (continued)		
		something in the pot, stir it, and put the lid back on). Gamelike routines such as Peekaboo typically follow a specific sequence of steps. If a parent says something like "We have to put these toys away first before we can get the other toys out," and then does that, it counts as a sequence of steps. Include counting and the order of book reading *only* when the parent is explicitly teaching how to count or how to look at a book.
7. Talks to child about characteristics of objects	Parent uses words or phrases that describe features such as color, shape, texture, movement, function, or other characteristics.	Characteristics of objects are described primarily by adjectives. Statements about function such as "Books are for reading" or "This is for listening to the heartbeat" are also about the characteristics of objects. When the parent says, "Dogs say 'woof,'" it is a functional characteristic of an object (but not explaining). Both variability and frequency are important. Saying "red" lots of times is not as clear as saying "big," "red," and "round." This item includes referring to the number of objects: "There are two lions." When the parent says the food the parent and child have just pretended to cook is hot, it can be both pretending and talking about characteristics of objects. When the parent talks about pictures in a book, the words may both label and talk about characteristics of objects (simply reading the words in a book does not count). Listen carefully because toys may bring out words about colors and shapes, but the words can also be used to describe the objects. For example, if a parent says, "Here's a square. Can you put it in the box?" the parent has labeled the objects, but the words were not used as descriptions. If the parent says, "It's a square block, and it goes in the square hole," then the parent is describing characteristics of the objects. Complexity and variety (color, shape, texture, function) count more.
8. Asks child for information	Parent asks any kind of question or says, "Tell me," "Show me," or other command that may require a yes/no response, short answer, or longer answer— whether or not child replies. Does not include questions to direct attention ("See?") or suggest activities ("Wanna open the bag?")	Questions must be asked in a way likely to elicit communication from the child, not just imitation. The parent must wait for an answer and appear to clearly expect an answer from the child. Questions that are truly asking for information are often repeated if the child does not reply right away. These questions do not include rhetorical questions, suggestions phrased as questions, or confirmation questions such as "Do you want to stir the pot?" or "It's a big spoon, isn't it?" Count either many simple questions such as "What's that?" or a few open-ended questions such as "Tell me about what you are building with these blocks," followed by encouraging prompts, such as "And what else?"

DOMAIN SUMMARIES

Sometimes it helps to understand what is generally known about each of these domains of parenting behavior. The following summary is based on information from *Developmental Parenting: A Guide for Early Childhood Practitioners,* a book written by two of the PICCOLO developers and another coauthor (Roggman et al., 2008).

Why Is Affection Important?

Affectionate parents express warmth and fondness toward their children. These parenting behaviors help children feel close and connected to their parents, and children are then more likely to be compliant and less likely to have tantrums and misbehave. A parent's affection provides a young child with a sense of being loved and cared for that lays a foundation for a positive relationship. These feelings help establish parent–child relationships that continue to support children's development, particularly their social and emotional development, from early in life through adolescence and into adulthood.

Frequent and consistent parenting interactions that are warm and affectionate lead to children being less likely to be noncompliant to parents' requests or to use misbehavior to get attention or control. Most children will misbehave or have temper tantrums at times, but when a child feels connected and loved, he or she is less likely to feel the sadness and anger that can lead to frequent and severe tantrums and misbehavior. A close relationship with the parent helps the child learn to express feelings, communicate about needs, try new skills, attempt new ways of communicating, and develop the self-regulation needed for behaving appropriately even when stressed, anxious, or frustrated. Affectionate interactions contribute to the kind of parent–child relationships that support children's development in all domains. When observing PICCOLO Affection behaviors, watch for indications that the behaviors express fondness and caring, promote connectedness, or reflect a positive relationship. Expect these behaviors to happen a little less as children get older.

Why Is Responsiveness Important?

Responsive parents understand what their child needs through the child's cues such as facial expressions, sounds and words, and movements, and they *consistently* respond to their children in ways that are helpful. When a parent is responsive, an infant learns to trust and forms a secure attachment, which provides a sense of trust and establishes an important foundation for social-emotional development. Infants who are securely attached, compared with those who are not, more often become children who are sociable, able to handle stress, and able to maintain positive relationships. A responsive parent offers comfort for physical distress by picking up a crying infant or feeding a hungry toddler. A responsive parent also reacts to a child's actions and replies to the child's expressions by sharing play and conversation.

Responsive parenting interactions not only support secure attachment but also often support the development of exploration and communication, other essential developmental foundations. A parent's helpful response when a toddler offers a toy or tries to get something just out of reach can support the child's exploration that underlies early cognitive development. When parents are responsive to children's cues, children are more likely to be confident and curious about the world. Responsive parents let their children take the lead in play, support exploration, and respond to children's early efforts to communicate with gestures and then language. When observing PICCOLO Responsiveness behaviors, watch for indications that the behaviors are specific to the child's expressions of needs or interests, are a good match with the child's current state, or promote trust.

Why Is Encouragement Important?

Encouragement involves letting the child explore, make choices, and use the beginning abilities of self-control. It supports a child's efforts to do new or challenging things. These parenting behaviors encourage children to persist or try something difficult or something they have not done before. Parents are encouraging when they help children learn to do things themselves.

Parents can be encouraging when they play together with children and toys. By being a playmate, a parent can encourage the child to lead the play activities by joining in with what the child does in play and by following along instead of taking over. Playing together in encouraging ways supports children's social skills and their developing cognitive skills. While playing with encouraging parents, children can learn to share toys and communicate about them. A parent can help make play more interesting or challenging if the child is getting bored or can offer assistance by gently scaffolding if the child is struggling to do something difficult. Parents can encourage initiative, curiosity, and creativity in their children's play by getting involved and supporting their children's interests without being intrusive. When observing PICCOLO Encouragement behaviors, watch for indications that the behaviors express support and enthusiasm, promote persistence, or help the child try new or difficult things.

Why Is Teaching Important?

Parents' early teaching interactions occur in the contexts of sharing conversation and play with infants. These interactions provide cognitive and language stimulation. Parents often chat with babies who cannot speak yet but look interested and make vocal sounds that will eventually become more speechlike. These somewhat one-sided conversations help children learn language. How much parents talk to their infants and how many different words they use will influence children's early language development. A child is more likely to begin to understand language if the parent pays attention to where the child is looking and talks about what the child sees. By sharing a child's focus of attention and providing a label for the shared experience, parents can encourage children's interests and curiosity and also provide language labels even before a child starts speaking any words. Infants begin understanding language earlier if their parents frequently label things, describe things, ask questions, answer questions, explain things, tell stories, and share books.

Even before the child can answer all of a parent's questions, questions that begin with *why, where, how,* or *who* will help children understand more language and begin to practice using their early language skills. By expanding on what the child says by repeating it and adding more words, a parent helps the child learn more language. Reading books, telling stories, sharing family routines, and pretending together all support language, cognitive development, and the beginnings of emergent literacy. When observing PICCOLO Teaching behaviors, watch for indications that the behaviors help a child learn something, expose a child to language and knowledge, or promote play or communication. Expect these behaviors to happen a little more as children get older.

ESTABLISHING PICCOLO™ RELIABILITY

Becoming reliable with PICCOLO is not a difficult process. The following steps lead to reliable observations.

How to Get Started

The easiest way to become reliable at PICCOLO observations is to begin with *The PICCOLO™ Training DVD*. First, watch the presentation, *PICCOLO: An Observational Measure of Developmental Parenting*, on the DVD. Then, practice observing one of the 1-minute or 5-minute video clips. It is best if at least two people observe the same video clip and then discuss their ratings. Watch the video clip, complete the PICCOLO measure, and then check your ratings with another person who watches the same clip.

After reviewing each video clip with another observer, discuss the differences in your ratings and come to an agreement on as many items as you can. Then, look up the ratings and rationale for each item in Appendix C. Watch the clip again to make sure you understand each of the ratings. Using the same process, work through all of the 1-minute and 5-minute video clips on *The PICCOLO™ Training DVD*.

After you have resolved any disagreements and are certain that you understand the ratings on the 1-minute and 5-minute video clips, try one of the 10-minute clips. Follow the same sequence, and work through all of the 10-minute video clips on the DVD.

We recommend that any program or research group using the PICCOLO make their own video clips for additional practice in their group over time. Sometimes an observer has observed and scored all of the video clips on *The PICCOLO™ Training DVD* but still needs more practice to agree with other observers. Video clips of local families may also help observers take into account cultural and regional variations in parenting behavior when they score PICCOLO observations.

The developers of PICCOLO are available to provide training workshops to help practitioners and researchers learn how to use, score, and apply PICCOLO.

Reliability Criteria

The minimum level of interrater agreement that we recommend for practitioner use is 75%. Generally, this means that there are no more than 3 items with a 1-point difference (or only 1 item with a 2-point difference and another with a 1-point difference) within any domain. Different uses of PICCOLO require different criteria for establishing reliability.

1. *For planning with families:* PICCOLO is used to identify parenting strengths, explore contexts when parents are most likely to use those strengths, and plan program activities such as home visit activities or group socialization activities that incorporate similar contexts. *Criteria for reliability:* Observers need an aware-

ness of PICCOLO developmental parenting behaviors and the ability to notice these multiple aspects of developmentally supportive parenting.

2. *For tracking family progress:* PICCOLO is used to measure developmentally supportive parenting at multiple time points to see which domains increase over time for individual families. This requires consistency over time in observational reliability. *Criteria for reliability:* Observers need within-rater agreement of more than 75% that is consistent over time.

3. *For improving your program:* PICCOLO is used to measure developmentally supportive parenting at the beginning and the end of the program to see which domains are strengths among the families served and which domains the program effectively increases. This requires that all the observers in your program are rating PICCOLO the same way. *Criteria for reliability:* Observers need within-rater and between-rater agreement of at least 75%.

4. *For evaluating program impact:* PICCOLO is used to measure developmentally supportive parenting at the beginning and the end of the program, particularly in comparison with families who do not receive the program, to test the program's impact in the context of research. This requires reliability to an external standard. *Criteria for reliability:* Observers need within-rater, between-rater, and between-site reliability of at least 75%. (This level of reliability typically requires additional expense to establish reliability with measurement developers.)

Chapter 3 provides information on conducting a PICCOLO observation.

3

Using PICCOLO™

The following questions provide clarification on conducting a PICCOLO observation.

How long should PICCOLO™ observations last?

PICCOLO observations need to be long enough to get a good sample of parenting interaction behaviors but short enough to complete as part of a home visit. We recommend a 10-minute observation, although a 5-minute observation usually can be reliably scored. A variety of activities can be used for PICCOLO observations. For PICCOLO observations of parenting interaction behaviors in all four domains, select a variety of activities that are likely to engage parents and children for at least 10 minutes.

What kinds of activities are good to use for PICCOLO™ observations?

Select activities that

- Fit program goals

- Can be done in a small space

- Engage both the parent and the child

- Last about 10 minutes

We have found that including a *variety* of activities allows opportunities for a variety of parenting interaction behaviors. It is good to offer choices of activities using toys and materials provided by the program, toys and materials the family already has, or a mix of materials with some from the home (familiar) and some from the program (variety).

Good activities should be appropriate for infants and young children and may include the following:

- Picture books with or without words (e.g., *Goodnight Moon* [Brown, 1947]; *Good Dog, Carl* [Day, 1985])

- Manipulative toys (e.g., puzzles, blocks, shape sorter), playdough, or art supplies

- Pretend play toys (e.g., cash register with toy foods, kitchen set, doll or stuffed animal, toy cars)

- Typical family routines (e.g., eating a meal, cleaning up)

- Planned home visit activities that involve the parents and children interacting together

How can I help families be comfortable being observed?

We have learned several tips from our program partner practitioners that increase the success of PICCOLO observations.

Tip 1.   Plan ahead and let families know you will be observing them and why. Explain the purpose of using the PICCOLO measure, and let parents know PICCOLO observations will be ongoing. If possible, involve the parents in planning the activities for the observation.

Tip 2.   Be flexible—if today turns out to be the wrong time, reschedule the observation for another time. If the child is sick, the family is having a crisis, or there are unusual or distracting circumstances in the home, reschedule for a time when the parent and child will be comfortable and behaving more typically.

Tip 3.   Do the observation where the family is comfortable—inside or outside, kitchen or living room or bedroom. Observations can also be done at program offices if there is a room similar to a kitchen or living room where parents can either sit on the floor or at a table with their child. Observations have also been done in center classrooms.

Tip 4.   If you video-record the observations, and we recommend that you do, watch the video together with the parent and child. Ask what the parent liked about playing together. Ask what else the parent would have liked to have done. The parent's answers will tell you about his or her goals for parenting and about the child's interests. You can then use this information to plan other activities to support positive parenting. Using PICCOLO can guide your discussion.

Tip 5.   Also, if you video-record the observations, offer families a copy of the video recording. It is a small reward for the experience and can offer an opportunity for the parent to observe and reflect on his or her own parenting interaction style.

When is the best time to score PICCOLO™?

There are several options for scoring the PICCOLO measure. We recommend scoring PICCOLO while, or immediately after, watching a video recording of the observation. Scoring from a video minimizes distractions from other events occurring near the observation setting and makes it possible to pause the observation if there is an interruption to the observer.

Another advantage of video is that practitioners can do the PICCOLO ratings alone, with the parent, or with a supervisor while reviewing the video recording. Some of the advantages of video observations are not only that parents can observe their own behaviors but also that observation is possible by someone who could not be present for the observation, such as a supervisor, mentor, or co-worker.

PICCOLO was developed by having observers watch a video observation one time before scoring, and PICCOLO items were selected for the measure based on being reliably observed from just one viewing of the video so that the demands of the observation would be similar to a live observation. We recommend scoring the video immediately after an observation. PICCOLO can therefore be used live by doing the ratings while watching the parent and child interacting. In this case, video recording is not required.

Some practitioners have done the observation on a home visit and then scored PICCOLO after the visit, but if there is much delay between the observation and the PICCOLO scoring, it will be difficult for the practitioner to remember the observation and score it accurately.

Is it important to score all four PICCOLO™ domains?

We recommend scoring all four domains of PICCOLO with families in order to be

- *Positive:* Most parents have strengths in more than one of the four domains.

- *Practical:* Practitioners can see more parenting strengths if they are watching for all four domains.

- *Culturally sensitive:* Different cultures emphasize different domains.

- *Sensible*: Using all four domains helps practitioners see the whole picture.

Is video-recording important?

Even if PICCOLO is used live, we recommend video-recording PICCOLO observations when possible. We have several reasons for making this recommendation.

1. Having a video recording of the observation allows practitioners to take time to pause the recording if interrupted or to check the observation guidelines when they are scoring PICCOLO.

2. Having a video recording allows practitioners to check the reliability of their scores by having someone else view the video either separately or together and discussing any disagreements about the scores.

3. Watching the video recording with the family offers rich opportunities to help parents identify their developmentally supportive parenting interactions themselves. Use PICCOLO to discuss the parent's behaviors that support his or her child's early development.

4. Making video recordings offers opportunities to reflect with a supervisor on this family's parenting strengths and needs.

5. Making and keeping video recordings over time helps practitioners in the same program become better observers by practicing more PICCOLO observations.

Note: If someone other than the family and practitioner will view the video recording, be sure to get written permission from the parent.

What are some tips for video-recording PICCOLO™ observations?

- Conduct the observation in a quiet place where the child and parent can interact without distractions. Ask the parent to turn off the television, radio, or other sound-producing devices. Avoid placing the camera near anything that makes noise, such as a fan, heater, or aquarium.

- Point the camera away from lights or windows. A light or window will make the camera adjust the exposure, and the parent and child you are trying to observe may be in the dark and difficult to see.

- Use a tripod to hold the video camera steady, or place the video camera on a solid object. Even if you hold a small camera very still, there will be wobbliness in the video that will make the video difficult to watch.

- Keep both the parent and the child in the viewfinder. For some parenting behaviors, it is important to know what the child is doing.

- Keep faces, hands, toys, and materials in the viewfinder. (You may need to ask a parent or child to remove a hat.) Emotional expressions, gestures, and the use of materials are all important for PICCOLO observations.

- Set a timer for 10 minutes. PICCOLO was developed using 10-minute observations. An observation at least 5 minutes long can be used to score PICCOLO, but 10 minutes is best.

- Keep watching to make sure everything stays in the viewfinder. Sometimes a camera slips, so it is important to check from time to time to make sure both the parent and child and their faces and hands remain visible, along with any toys or other materials they use.

- Try to be as unobtrusive as possible, and do not interrupt or engage in the interaction. It may be helpful to be reading or writing something that takes your eyes away from the interaction, but be sure to check the camera occasionally.

SCORING PICCOLO™

The following section provides clarification on the scoring process.

How do I score PICCOLO™?

- Add the item scores in each domain to get a domain score; add the domain scores to get a total PICCOLO score.

- Look at higher scores, by domain and by item, as strengths.

- Consider other information about the parent, child, and family.

- Talk with the parent about his or her perceptions of observed interactions with the child.

- Be aware that these scores are based on a low-income diverse sample.

The scoring grids in Figure 3.1 show the range of scores in each domain with the darkest shades indicating strengths.

How should I interpret PICCOLO™ scores?

The best way to interpret PICCOLO scores is by looking at the high domain scores or high item scores as parenting strengths. Almost all parents do some positive things when interacting with their children, and the PICCOLO measure will help practitioners identify these behaviors. Higher scores indicate more developmentally supportive parenting behaviors, but every parent will have strengths in some items

Affection domain scores

1 year old	0	1	2	3	4	5	6	7	8	9	10	11	12	13	14
2 years old	0	1	2	3	4	5	6	7	8	9	10	11	12	13	14
3 years old	0	1	2	3	4	5	6	7	8	9	10	11	12	13	14

Responsiveness domain scores

1 year old	0	1	2	3	4	5	6	7	8	9	10	11	12	13	14
2 years old	0	1	2	3	4	5	6	7	8	9	10	11	12	13	14
3 years old	0	1	2	3	4	5	6	7	8	9	10	11	12	13	14

Encouragement domain scores

1 year old	0	1	2	3	4	5	6	7	8	9	10	11	12	13	14
2 years old	0	1	2	3	4	5	6	7	8	9	10	11	12	13	14
3 years old	0	1	2	3	4	5	6	7	8	9	10	11	12	13	14

Teaching domain scores

1 year old	0	1	2	3	4	5	6	7	8	9	10	11	12	13	14	15	16
2 years old	0	1	2	3	4	5	6	7	8	9	10	11	12	13	14	15	16
3 years old	0	1	2	3	4	5	6	7	8	9	10	11	12	13	14	15	16

Figure 3.1. Parenting Interactions with Children: Checklist of Observations Linked to Outcomes (PICCOLO™) scoring grids by domain. (*Key:* □ below average scores; ▦ average scores; ■ above average scores.)

or domains compared with other items or domains. Practitioners can use parent strengths to expand or scaffold parenting behaviors that could be made stronger.

Sometimes, however, practitioners need an idea about when a low score indicates risk for parenting problems or poor child outcomes. For these situations, we have developed scoring grids, shown in Figure 3.1. These grids show how PICCOLO scores varied across families in our measurement sample. For each domain, we have identified which scores are average (shown in light gray), higher than average (highest 16% of scores, shown in dark gray), and lower than average (lowest 16% of scores, shown in white). Low PICCOLO domain scores are associated with lower scores on assessments of children's cognitive, language, and social development. Low scores indicate that the parent and child are having difficulty engaging with each other in ways that support the child's development.

Total PICCOLO scores, summing across domain scores, ranged from a minimum score of 6 to a maximum score of 58, with above average scores (highest 16% of scores) over 47 at age 14 months and over 49 at ages 24 and 36 months and below average scores (lowest 16% of scores) under 31 at 14 months and under 33 at 24 and 36 months. Among the over 2,000 families in our PICCOLO sample, no parents scored 0 on the total PICCOLO score.

Remember, these scores are based on a diverse low-income sample and are therefore similar to the range of scores that are likely to be observed in families served by programs such as Early Head Start. Higher scores would be expected as socioeconomic factors, such as parent education, increase and environmental stressors, such as from poverty, decrease.

USING PICCOLO™ WITH FAMILIES

The following section provides ideas for using PICCOLO with families.

What are some ideas for using PICCOLO™ information with families?

When using PICCOLO information with parents, be positive, practical, culturally sensitive, and sensible. Keep your eye on the prize by remembering that the goal is to promote children's development, so the purpose of the PICCOLO measure is to identify ways that parents are promoting development in their interactions with their children. PICCOLO can help practitioners avoid the strategies of demonstrating a "correct" way to interact with children or showing off their skills, strategies that may alienate parents instead of engaging them with their own children. Instead, PICCOLO helps emphasize parents' strengths in interacting with their children, which is a goal of many home visiting programs.

- *Be positive:* Emphasize parenting strengths by focusing on what a parent does well and often. Some parents may score consistently across items and domains, whereas others may have more uneven profiles. Some parents may have strengths in certain parenting behaviors or in certain parenting domains. Their parenting strengths would be indicated by particular PICCOLO items on which parents score higher than on other items or by particular PICCOLO domains on which parents score higher than on other domains.

- *Be practical:* Build on parents' strengths by asking *when* they can do more of the PICCOLO behaviors they already do and *how* they can begin doing some that they do not do as much. A parent may do more PICCOLO behaviors at certain times of the day, during particular family routines, or during other activities. These times offer opportunities for parents to expand their support of children's early development by increasing their use of behaviors they already do and by trying similar behaviors in the same domain. These contexts also offer opportunities for parents to try new behaviors in other domains by using their strengths in one domain, such as the Teaching domain, to try a similar behavior in another domain, such as by being more responsive to children's sounds or words, a behavior in the Responsiveness domain.

- *Be culturally sensitive:* Be sensitive to parents' culture and values by asking what kinds of parenting interactions are important to them. What parents do in their interactions with their children, especially when they are being observed, are those parenting behaviors they value and believe are important to do. Ask for more information if the parent interacts in ways that are not familiar to you. By helping parents reflect on their reasons for doing what they do with their children, practitioners can help parents express their values and the expectations of their culture. For example, "You show a lot of affection to your child. Why is that important to you?" or "Does it help when you encourage him to try things?"

- *Be sensible:* Understand parenting strengths in the context of other information about each family. Many characteristics of a parent and family may influence a parent's interaction with a child, such as the number of other children in the family, the parent's age and education, financial stress, whether the parent works or is in school, or the parent's mental and physical health. Use this knowledge to guide your encouragement of parents' strengths.

How can PICCOLO™ information be used to improve services to families?

PICCOLO scores reveal parents' strengths. The domains in which parents are strongest will be the best place to start building their overall capacity to support their children's development. Something that a parent is already doing will be the easiest parenting behavior to increase so that parents can more effectively support their children's early development.

Parenting strengths in one domain can sometimes be used to increase their strengths in another domain, a process we call *bridging* because it requires the practitioner to make connections between domains. For example, if a parent shows a lot of affection but does little teaching, a practitioner can focus on increasing the parent's affectionate interactions and then use these interactions to bridge to teaching by helping the parent think of ways to include more talking as part of their affection, perhaps by being more detailed in their praise of the child or using a wider variety of words to express affection. The parent can then gradually begin to add more teaching to his or her parenting interactions in a way that will come naturally and feel comfortable.

Information about a parent's strengths can guide the planning process. These strengths can guide the selection of activities for home visits or other parenting consultations. Activities that incorporate parenting behaviors indicated as strengths in PICCOLO scores are more likely to be successful at engaging parents in interactions that help their children's development. And parents are more likely to follow suggestions for parenting activities with children between sessions if those suggestions take into account behaviors the parent is most likely to do. By encouraging parents to use their strengths, practitioners can more effectively help parents support their children's development in ways that are comfortable and likely to continue.

How can PICCOLO™ information be used to improve programs for families?

PICCOLO information can improve programs for parents. PICCOLO scores can be averaged across families in an entire program, in different program components, or in different communities, for example. PICCOLO scores can be examined over time to identify parents who increase their use of developmentally supportive behaviors. By using PICCOLO scores as an outcome measure, the information can help guide improvements to the entire program.

A program can use PICCOLO information to answer questions such as the following:

- What are the most common strengths among parents in the whole program?

- How do parenting strengths vary across different communities or subgroups?

- How can these strengths be used to plan successful program activities?

- How do program services match the strengths of families in the program?

- How many parents improve their PICCOLO scores over the course of the program?

- Which PICCOLO domain improves most among the families in the program?

A program can also use PICCOLO information to identify training needs and resources of staff.

- Which domains do staff members understand best?

- Which domains do staff members believe are most important for their families?

- How well are parenting interventions working?

- Do program staff members need more observation skill practice?

- Do program staff members need more intervention ideas?

USING PICCOLO™ WITH CHILDREN WHO ARE OLDER, YOUNGER, OR HAVE DISABILITIES

We recommend PICCOLO for observing parents with children ages 10–47 months because that is the age range for which we have the most data and the largest sample. The reliability and validity data for PICCOLO are based on observations of parents interacting with children ranging in age from 10 months to 47 months. Our data show promise, however, for using PICCOLO to observe parents with children older than age 47 months or with infants younger than 10 months and to observe parents of children with disabilities.

Older Children

For older children, we have tested PICCOLO on observations of parents from a subset of the same sample as the original PICCOLO validation sample. The families in this subset were observed when their children were about to begin kindergarten, ranging in age from 52 to 73 months, with ⅔ of the children older than 60 months (5 years). PICCOLO was coded on this subsample of 136 mothers observed playing with their children with age-appropriate toys in a situation similar to the one used for the observations of parents with children ages 1–3 years.

Interrater agreement on PICCOLO scores with this older group averaged 76% overall, ranging from 73% to 83% across domains. Internal consistency alpha was .92 overall, ranging from .69 to .85 across domains. Construct validity was shown by a correlation of .54 between PICCOLO and independently coded parent supportiveness in another situation observed at the same time, ranging from .37 to .55 across domains. Some predictive validity is indicated by statistically significant correlations between one or more PICCOLO domains at age 5 with concurrent measures of attention and emergent literacy and at Grade 5 with better scores on measures of peer relations and social behavior. Generally, parents had higher average scores in the Teaching domain with this older group of children and lower scores in the other domains, compared with parents of younger children.

The data from these observations show that PICCOLO can be used for observing parents with children up to age 5, but the limitations of the sample size and outcome data suggest that the measure should be used with caution with parents of older children, and different meanings of interactions with children who are further developed should be carefully considered.

Younger Infants

For parenting with younger infants, 4–9 months old, careful consideration should be given to how parents do similar behaviors with children who are not mobile and do not understand much language. Recently, we have been encouraged by practitioners who have adapted the items for use with parents of infants as young as 4 months by describing how each behavior could be expressed with younger infants. Our observations of a limited number of video observations of parents with infants 4–9 months suggest that PICCOLO can be used reliably in this age range, with the appropriate modifications to definitions and expectations.

We are continuing research with a larger number of observations to determine whether PICCOLO can be scored reliably from observations of parents interacting with infants 4–9 months and to determine whether PICCOLO scores at these younger ages predict either later PICCOLO scores or child outcomes. Until additional observation notes can be refined and reliability and validity can be established for PICCOLO with parents of younger infants, we urge caution in its use with this group.

Children with Disabilities

The sample used to develop PICCOLO had approximately 10% of the children receiving early intervention services or having a diagnosed disability that would have qualified them for services (Peterson et al., 2004). Data from this subsample of 188 mothers interacting with their children with disabilities at ages 14, 24, and 36 months, demonstrated the validity of PICCOLO scores for this group.

Construct validity was demonstrated in this subsample by statistically significant correlations, averaging .57, between PICCOLO and the ratings of overall parent supportiveness independently coded using a different measure from the same observations. Predictive validity was demonstrated by statistically significant correlations between PICCOLO and child outcomes, particularly for cognitive and language outcomes, averaging .24 when children were age 36 months and .31 when children were about to enter kindergarten.

USING PICCOLO™ WITH FATHERS (PICCOLO™-D)

The psychometric properties of PICCOLO have been tested by observing over 400 ethnically diverse fathers, from the same sample as the original PICCOLO validation sample, interacting with children ages 13–47 months. Of the original PICCOLO items, 21 items demonstrated strong psychometric properties when used to observe fathers. PICCOLO items *not* included in the research on fathers were Item 4 (physically close) and Item 5 (positive expressions) from the Affection domain, Item 3 (flexible) and Item 6 (looks when child makes sounds) from the Responsiveness domain, Item 1 (waits) and Item 6 (suggestions to help) from the Encouragement domain, and Item 1 (explains) and Item 6 (activities in a sequence) from the Teaching domain.

Interrater agreement for these 21 items, referred to as PICCOLO-D (for dads), was tested with newly trained undergraduate observers on 113 randomly selected observations. Agreement averaged 71% overall, ranging from 68% to 75% across domains ($N = 512$ observations). Internal consistency Cronbach's alpha, using the case average across the three child ages, was .91 for the full measure and ranged from .66 for the Teaching domain to .81 for the Responsiveness domain ($N = 428$ observations).

Construct validity, using the case average across the three child ages, is evident in a correlation of .66 between PICCOLO-D and independently coded parent supportiveness of the same observations, ranging from .51 to .61 across domains with respective measures for each domain (e.g., positive regard with Affection). Statistically significant correlations for children's language outcomes at age 3 and at prekindergarten with PICCOLO-D scores at child ages 1, 2, and 3 years ranged from .23 ($n = 217$) for PICCOLO-D at child age 3 with prekindergarten receptive vocabulary to .36 ($n = 58$) for PICCOLO-D at child age 1 predicting age 3 receptive vocabulary. For children's cognitive outcomes, at age 3 and at prekindergarten, statistically significant correlations with PICCOLO-D scores at child ages 1, 2, and 3 years ranged from .22, ($n = 221$) for PICCOLO-D at child age 3 with concurrent cognitive outcomes to .33 ($n = 223$) with PICCOLO-D at child age 2 predicting age 3 cognitive outcomes. For children's social-emotional outcomes, statistically significant correlations ranged from .16 ($n = 211$) for PICCOLO-D at child age 3 with prekindergarten emotion regulation to .26 ($n = 225$) for PICCOLO-D at child age 2 predicting prekindergarten emotion regulation.

We would not discourage practitioners from providing positive feedback to fathers on the other PICCOLO items that were deleted from PICCOLO-D. All PICCOLO items demonstrated good content validity supported by documentation in published research studies of father–child interaction and by ratings of importance for child development by father research experts. Also, we would not encourage practitioners to use only the reduced set of items with mothers because analyses on the reduced set of items for mothers did not show evidence of the same levels of reliability and validity as the full original set of 29 PICCOLO items.

Additional considerations may be needed for observing fathers. For example, some items, such as *warm tone of voice* and *smiles*, had slightly lower percent agreement when observed with fathers. Observers described fathers as less frequently using higher pitched tones of voice with children, compared with mothers. For fathers, observers learned to listen more for "interest" and "enjoyment." Observers also found that when fathers had facial hair or wore hats, smiles were more difficult to observe. Fathers are, on average, physically larger than mothers, so they may need more space for playing with their children.

Practitioners using PICCOLO-D with fathers indicated that it was helpful for tailoring curriculum to meet the needs of diverse families, for engaging fathers in home visits, and for supporting parents in negotiating coparenting. Some practitioners used their knowledge of PICCOLO-D items to encourage positive father–child interaction during home visits. Others offered the PICCOLO-D observation as a choice of activities that the father could do during a home visit. Overall, practitioners found that using PICCOLO-D helped them notice and encourage positive behaviors, which facilitated trust and engagement by fathers.

Chapter 4 answers more questions that practitioners have asked about the PICCOLO.

4

Practitioner Questions About PICCOLO™ (Frequently Asked Questions)

Practitioners have asked questions about the PICCOLO observational measure. Here are answers to some of those questions.

Are the behaviors in PICCOLO™ subjective?

The term *subjective* generally means that a behavior is seen differently by different people. We used the level of agreement among multiple observers to select items that different people usually see the same way.

Items seen differently by different people most likely require too much subjective interpretation (e.g., "Parent enjoys being with child"). PICCOLO items avoid the need for interpretation by describing behaviors and providing observation guidelines for each item. Observers agreed less on some original items than on others, so the items with low agreement were eliminated from the measure.

We refined the wording and definitions of several items to be more observable and less open to bias. Initial wording for many items was taken from the wording of measures in parenting research articles. Wording changes increased the objectivity and agreement for several items. In reality, we all have different lenses with which we view others' behaviors, but we increased the objectivity of PICCOLO by using more observable items ("Parent smiles at child") and decreased the subjectivity by deleting less observable items ("Parent is comfortable with child").

PICCOLO includes the best set of items that different observers rate the same way and that also predict child outcomes. The fact that observers quickly become reliable means PICCOLO is not too subjective. PICCOLO is therefore useful for practitioners looking for a reliable and valid way to measure parenting interactions.

Is a 3-point scale too general?

PICCOLO items use a 3-point rating scale, from 0 (*absent,* or no evidence of the behavior) to 1 (*barely,* or some brief, minor, or emerging behavior) to 2 (*clearly,* or definite, strong, or frequent behavior). When the item ratings are added up, parents vary quite a bit on total domain scores. This rating scale is similar to a checklist of behaviors with a yes/no response—quite common in well-known measures of behavior—except that an in-between rating point is allowed for behaviors that show some evidence of emergence even though they do not appear to be behaviors that are typical of that parent.

Because a characteristic such as responsiveness can be expressed in different ways at different times, the same total domain score from different behaviors can predict equally good outcomes for children. The PICCOLO domain scores predict children's outcomes across families, across ethnic groups, and across age groups. By having multiple item indicators of each domain, each domain becomes a more accurate measure of that category of behavior.

The advantage of PICCOLO's 3-point scale is that it is easy to score short observations (10 minutes or so) without counting or timing behaviors. This makes it possible for practitioners to score PICCOLO live during home visits or other observation opportunities.

A 4- or 5-point scale would make the PICCOLO measure more difficult to use, more difficult to teach, and more vulnerable to bias. When raters have a longer scale, they sometimes use more information, often from experiences outside the observation, to make their ratings. Our previous research with a different measure showed that scores based on a 9-point response scale were highly correlated with scores based on a response scale that had only 3 points.

Does PICCOLO™ make assumptions about what is a good or bad behavior?

The selection of items for the PICCOLO measure was based on parenting behaviors identified in research studies as predictors of child outcomes. We eliminated negative items and included only positive parenting behaviors linked to positive child outcomes in either cognitive-language development or social-emotional development.

We make no assumptions about the value of these behaviors, simply that they predict better developmental outcomes for children. The validity data on PICCOLO indicate that our measure is indeed valid because the parenting behaviors in the four domains in this measure predict better language vocabulary scores, better cognitive composite scores, and better behavior scores in young children.

How can PICCOLO™ be objective if the rater knows the family?

Objective observations require the avoidance of observer bias. Observer bias can occur not only from knowing a family but also from a variety of other sources of bias, such as halo effects, stereotypes, similarity, or attractiveness. All observers are likely to expect more good behaviors from someone they have already seen doing something good, the *halo effect*. Observers are also likely to expect behaviors consistent with their stereotypes related to age, ethnicity, attractiveness, and other aspects of appearance. They are likely to expect behavior similar to their own from someone similar to them.

For all of these reasons, it is important for those learning to use PICCOLO to practice observing and see if their observations agree with others. That is why we selected PICCOLO items based on agreement between raters. Items that could elicit more bias by requiring more subjective interpretation had lower agreement between raters and were eliminated from the final measure.

From our work with programs serving families with young children, we have found that practitioners can learn to record PICCOLO ratings based on the behavior they see during a specific time period rather than what they already think about a family. Practitioners vary, of course, in how well they are able to do that, and some need more practice than others. For these reasons, we strongly recommend video-recording observations so that an observer's objectivity can be tested by comparing ratings with another observer who does not know the family.

To detect change over time (e.g., increases in parents' teaching interactions with their children) in an objective way, we recommend restricting the ratings to observations of equal duration, preferably short enough to observe live or to video-record and review later—about 10 minutes. If practitioners use additional information to make the ratings (i.e., from what they have experienced with the family before the observation), their ratings will not be as useful to compare with later ratings after they know the family longer. Ratings can be accurately compared only if made from the same length of observation.

How can a practitioner use the information from PICCOLO™? If a parent does not smile at her infant, do we say, "You should smile now"? Will this be intrusive?

These are important questions that apply to parenting programs regardless of the assessment tools used. The researchers on this project have had many years of experience working with parenting programs, and many practitioners ask similar questions. What can they do to help parents support their children's development? How can they increase parents' warmth, responsiveness, encouragement, and communication with their children—the main aspects of parenting that research shows are related to better child outcomes?

PICCOLO items are observable behaviors that indicate affection, responsiveness, encouragement, and teaching. Practitioners can use their observations to build family strengths by talking about the positive behaviors parents are already doing and helping parents increase those behaviors and add other similar behaviors to their interactions with their young children.

Encouraging a parent to respond to an infant's smile by smiling back is not a bad idea. Sometimes parents are not aware of the effects of their expressions on their children, and helping them acknowledge children's positive behaviors may reinforce positive parenting. For example, a practitioner could ask, "How do you feel when she smiles at you like she just did?" or "Did you see him smile at you?"

Whether the message is intrusive or respectful, critical or supportive, offensive or friendly will depend on the practitioner's skills, which are unrelated to this measure. Although a variety of different kinds of programs may find the PICCOLO measure useful, we recommend an approach that is responsive to family strengths and culture, flexible in strategies, and supportive of each parent.

Why are negative behaviors not included? Are negative parenting interactions important to observe?

Yes, of course negative behaviors are important to observe, but there are several reasons we do not include negative interactions in PICCOLO. Negative items reduced the usefulness of PICCOLO. We tested some "red flag" items in each domain that would indicate negative interactions. Practitioners who tried early versions of PICCOLO found that it made the measure harder to use with parents. Our goal was to develop a measure that would help practitioners provide positive feedback to parents about their parenting strengths, and negative items would have undermined that goal. We designed PICCOLO for practitioners to use to recognize parents' strengths. Practitioners can then build on these strengths by identifying behaviors the parent clearly already does and encouraging more of those behaviors.

Sometimes practitioners need extra guidance to observe any positive interactions, especially when they are also seeing negative interactions. Negative interactions certainly have an impact, but practitioners usually do not have difficulty seeing them, are often uncomfortable pointing them out, and sometimes find parents to be defensive or unresponsive in discussions of their negative interactions.

Sometimes, however, negative interactions are not obvious. Subtle negative interactions are likely to vary in their meaning and impact depending on ethnicity or culture. A behavior that may seem negative or harsh may have a different meaning to observers who are not part of that same ethnicity or culture compared with its meaning for those in the same ethnic or cultural group as the parent being observed. For example, Ispa and her colleagues (2004) showed that mothers' intrusive behaviors, as rated by objective researchers, were not related to negative outcomes for African American children, even though they were for other ethnicity groups.

Finally, the negative items that we tested rarely occurred during video observations. This probably is because parents are on their best behavior when being observed, just like anyone is when, for example, taking a test or being interviewed by a journalist. This is not a bad thing because PICCOLO shows what parents believe is important to do as their best behavior as a parent. Parents are unlikely to do anything they do not believe is important or that they are not able to do in everyday interactions with their children. Anything you observe a parent doing, even just a little bit, is something the parents could increase to provide more developmental support for the child.

It may be useful for practitioners to have a list of red flags to watch out for, at least in their minds, but not as part of PICCOLO. We believe PICCOLO is more valuable as a measure that is appropriate to use side by side with parents to build their parenting strengths.

Can PICCOLO™ be used as a questionnaire or survey instrument to ask parents what they do with their children?

No, PICCOLO was not designed or tested for that purpose. Nevertheless, it might be an interesting exercise to ask parents which behaviors they find important to engage in with their children. Such an activity could help a practitioner who is learning more about a family get to know the family better by asking about a parent's beliefs or how a child responds. For example, a practitioner could ask a parent what a behavior means to him or her or could ask how his or her child reacts to a certain parental behavior.

Can PICCOLO™ scores be used in custody disputes or placement decisions? Can PICCOLO™ be used to identify neglectful parents? Can PICCOLO™ be used to decide raises for home visitors?

No, we do not recommend PICCOLO for these uses. PICCOLO has not been developed or tested for these uses, and it would be inappropriate to use PICCOLO for any high-stakes decision-making purpose.

We hope these answers to practitioners' questions have clarified how PICCOLO is used. Chapter 5 provides background information on how PICCOLO was developed.

5

How Was PICCOLO™ Developed?

PICCOLO was developed to provide a useful observational measure of positive parenting for practitioners working with parents of young children. It was developed to be reliable and valid as well as practical. Practitioners at our multiple program partners were involved in the development of PICCOLO at each step. The research team used practitioner feedback to select and refine PICCOLO items and to develop suggestions for the use of the measure with families.

MEASUREMENT DEVELOPMENT PROCESS

Step 1.   The research team reviewed the research literature to identify parenting interaction domains and specific parenting behavior descriptors that were related to children's developmental outcomes. After this review, short phrases describing research-based parenting behaviors were identified in four domains: Affection, Responsiveness, Encouragement, and Teaching.

Behavior descriptions of parenting linked to positive child outcomes were used to create an initial list of parenting behavior indicators to be tested. This list was reviewed by the research team to eliminate items that were unclear, vague, or not observable. To assess content validity, items on this list were rated for importance by practitioners in infant-toddler/early childhood programs. New observers tested a reduced list of potential items for the measure using an archive of video observations from the Early Head Start Research and Evaluation Project.

Step 2.   New observers independently viewed and rated over 4,500 video recordings of parenting interactions using the item descriptors. They received regular quantitative feedback on their levels of agreement and provided qualitative feedback on items to the research team.

To select the items for PICCOLO, parenting behaviors were defined in easily observable terms and tested by new observers viewing an archive of video recordings of parenting interactions with children ages 10–47 months. New observers received basic information and training comparable to what a new practitioner would receive in an infant-toddler/early childhood program. At least three observers viewed each video clip and rated the PICCOLO items on each video observation of parent–child interaction.

The archive of video-recorded observations included families from European American, African American, and Latino American groups. Most of the families had low incomes and had been enrolled in the research sample of the national Early Head Start Research and Evaluation Project.

Initial coding teams were matched by ethnicity but later assigned to cross–ethnic group coding. Multiple criteria were met across all three ethnic groups for each selected item. For interrater reliability analyses, at least two coders rated every observation. For predictive validity analyses, at least two coders rated every observation.

Step 3.   The research team used multiple criteria to select final items based on

- Interrater reliability of each item
- Scale reliability within each domain
- Construct validity with extant parenting data
- Predictive validity with extant child outcome data
- Family variability
- Intercorrelations between items
- Content validity from importance ratings
- Ease of use from practitioner feedback on item clarity
- Other qualitative feedback from raters and partners

A final set of items was selected for PICCOLO based on these multiple criteria. A single factor structure was examined for each domain, and the interrelatedness of items within each domain indicated that the items were measuring the same underlying construct.

To assess construct validity, PICCOLO ratings from these observations were analyzed in relation to similar dimensions of parent–child interactions independently measured from the same observations. To assess predictive validity, PICCOLO ratings were analyzed in relation to children's developmental outcomes. Reliability and validity data are reported in the PICCOLO Technical Report in Appendix A.

Step 4.   To assess practical validity, practitioners from three intervention programs used PICCOLO with families in their programs. Training on the use of the measure was provided to practitioners in two home-based Early Head Start programs and one other infant-toddler home visiting program. Together with these program partners, the research team assessed the usefulness of PICCOLO for practitioners. Researchers developed PICCOLO observation procedures for practitioners and got practitioner feedback on ease of use, meaningfulness, and appropriateness of the measure for the families served by the partner programs.

Each stage of the development of PICCOLO was enriched by our collaboration with practitioners working with parents of infants, toddlers, and young children. Practitioners tried out early versions of the PICCOLO items and provided feedback about the clarity and importance of each item. Practitioners provided ideas about what kinds of parenting interactions they thought were important, ratings of the importance and clarity for each item, and qualitative feedback on items in the early versions of the measure. Practitioners' feedback on the training materials used during the project guided the development of materials for dissemination to other practitioners who will use the PICCOLO measure.

Step 5.   After the partner programs had used the measure with multiple families, the research team met with practitioners to develop guidelines for PICCOLO use. Practitioners provided ideas about the best situations for conducting PICCOLO observations, the best approaches for when and how to code the items, and the best uses of the data afterward. Practitioners in our partner programs also provided suggestions for the training materials that would be available to other practitioners. Focus groups provided ideas and video recordings of practitioners discussing the PICCOLO measure.

Practitioners provided detailed descriptions of how they used the measure with families. They provided extensive feedback about ways to use PICCOLO effectively with parents on home visits and ways to use PICCOLO as a guide for intervention activities with families in home visiting programs. Practitioners have used PICCOLO collaboratively with parents to review and reflect on video recordings of their interactions with their infants, toddlers, and young children.

Step 6.   The research team developed training, support, and documentation materials that include the PICCOLO measure with observation guidelines, this user's guide, a technical report (Appendix A), and *The PICCOLO™ Training DVD: Implementation and Scoring* (Roggman et al., 2013), which includes training information and video clips for observation practice. Scores and rationale for the video clips on *The PICCOLO™ Training DVD* are available in Appendix C. Finally, the translation of PICCOLO into several other languages began and is continuing. The Spanish version of PICCOLO is available in Appendix B.

These steps have resulted in a tool that is not only psychometrically sound as a research measure but accessible and useful for practitioners to identify and support developmental parenting behaviors.

References

Achenbach, T.M., & Rescorla, L.A. (2000). *Manual for ASEBA preschool forms and profiles.* Burlington: University of Vermont, Research Center for Children, Youth and Families.

Administration for Children and Families. (2002). *Making a difference in the lives of infants and toddlers and their families: The impact of Early Head Start. Vol. II: Final technical report appendices.* Washington, DC: U.S. Department of Health and Human Services.

Barnard, K.E., & Kelly, J. (1990). *Assessment of mother–child interaction.* New York, NY: Cambridge University Press.

Barnard, K.E., Morisset, C.E., & Spieker, S. (1993). Preventive interventions: Enhancing parent–infant relationships. In C. Zeanah (Ed.), *Handbook of infant mental health* (pp. 386–401). New York, NY: Guilford Press.

Bayley, N. (1993). *Bayley Scales of Infant Development: Mental Development Index and Behavior Rating Scale.* San Antonio, TX: Psychological Corp.

Berlin, L.J., Brady-Smith, C., & Brooks-Gunn, J. (2002). Links between childbearing age and observed maternal behaviors with 14-month-olds in the Early Head Start Research and Evaluation Project. *Infant Mental Health Journal, 23,* 104–129.

Bernier, A., Carlson, S.M., & Whipple, N. (2010). From external regulation to self-regulation: Early parenting precursors of young children's executive functioning. *Child Development, 81,* 326–339.

Bernstein, V.J., Campbell, S., & Akers, A. (2001). Caring for the caregivers: Supporting the well-being of at-risk parents and children through supporting the well-being of the programs that serve them. In J. Hughes, J. Close, & A. La Greca (Eds.), *Handbook of psychological services for children and adolescents* (pp. 107–131). New York, NY: Oxford University Press.

Bernstein, V.J., Hans, S.L., & Percansky, C. (1991). Advocating for the young child in need through strengthening the parent–child relationship. *Journal of Child Clinical Psychology, 20,* 28–41.

Bingham, G. (2007). Maternal literacy beliefs and the quality of mother–child book reading interactions: Associations with children's early literacy development. *Early Education and Development, 18,* 23–49.

Booth, C.L., Rose-Krasnor, L., McKinnon, J., & Rubin, K.H. (1994). Predicting social adjustment in middle childhood: The role of preschool attachment security and maternal style. *Social Development, 3*(3), 189–204.

Brady-Smith, C., Fauth, R., & Brooks-Gunn, J. (2005). *Early Head Start research and evaluation project: Background and psychometric information for the child–parent interaction rating scales for the three-bag assessment 14-, 24-, and 36-month waves.* New York, NY: Columbia University.

Brotman, L., O'Neal, C.R., Keng-Yen, H., Gouley, K., Rosenfelt, A., & Shrout, P.E. (2009). An experimental test of parenting practices as a mediator of early childhood physical aggression. *Journal of Child Psychology & Psychiatry, 50*(3), 235–245.

Brown, M. (1947). *Goodnight moon.* New York, NY: Harper & Row.

Caldwell, B.M., & Bradley, R.H. (1984). *Home Observation for Measurement of the Environment (HOME).* Little Rock: University of Arkansas.

Caspi, A., Moffitt, T.E., Morgan, J., Rutter, M., Taylor, A., Arseneault, L., ... Polo-Tomas, M. (2004). Maternal expressed emotion predicts children's antisocial behavior problems: Using monozygotic-twin differences to identify environmental effects on behavioral development. *Developmental Psychology, 40*, 149–161.

Culp, A.M., Hubbs-Tait, L., Culp, R.E., & Starost, H.J. (2000). Maternal parenting characteristics and school involvement: Predictors of kindergarten cognitive competence among Head Start children. *Journal of Research in Childhood Education, 15*(1), 5–17.

Davidov, M., & Grusec, J.E. (2006). Untangling the links of parental responsiveness to distress and warmth to child outcomes. *Child Development, 77*, 44–58.

Day, A. (1985). *Good dog, Carl.* New York, NY: Simon & Schuster.

Dodici, B.J., Draper, D.C., & Peterson, C.A. (2003). Early parent–child interactions and early literacy development. *Topics in Early Childhood Special Education, 23*, 124–136.

Dunn, L.M., & Dunn, L.M. (1997). *Peabody Picture Vocabulary Test–Third Edition (PPVT-III).* Circle Pines, MN: American Guidance Service.

Estrada, P., Arsenio, W.F., Hess, R.D., & Holloway, S.D. (1987). Affective quality of the mother–child relationship: Longitudinal consequences of children's school-relevant cognitive functioning. *Developmental Psychology, 23*, 210–215.

Farah, M.J., Betancourt, L., Shera, D.M., Savage, J.H., Giannetta, J.M., Brodsky, N.L.,...& Hurt, H. (2008). Environmental stimulation, parental nurturance and cognitive development in humans. *Developmental Science, 11*(5), 793–801.

Fenson, L., Dale, P.S., Reznick, J.S., Bates, E., Thal, D.J., Pethick, S.J., ... & Stiles, J. (1994). Variability in early communicative development. *Monographs of the Society for Research in Child Development*, 1–185.

Fewell, R.R., & Deutscher, B. (2002). Contributions of receptive vocabulary and maternal style variables to later verbal ability and reading in low-birthweight children. *Topics in Early Childhood Special Education, 22*(4), 181–190.

Frodi, A., Bridges, L., & Grolnick, W. (1985). Correlates of mastery-related behavior: A short-term longitudinal study of infants in their second year. *Child Development, 56*, 1291–1298.

Fuligni, A.S., & Brooks-Gunn, J. (2013). Mother–child interactions in Early Head Start: Age and ethnic differences in low-income dyads. *Parenting, 13*(1), 1–26.

Gardner, F., Ward, S., Burton, J., & Wilson, C. (2003). The role of mother–child joint play in the early development of children's conduct problems: A longitudinal observational study. *Social Development, 12*(3), 361–378.

Goldberg, S. (1977). Social competence in infancy: A model of parent–infant interaction. *Merrill-Palmer Quarterly: Journal of Developmental Psychology, 29*, 163–177.

Green, B.L., McAllister, C.L., & Tarte, J.M. (2005). The Strengths-Based Practices Inventory: A tool for measuring strengths-based service delivery in early childhood and family support programs. *Families in Society, 85*(3), 326–334.

Hart, B., & Risley, T.R. (1995). *Meaningful differences in the everyday experience of young American children.* Baltimore, MD: Paul H. Brookes Publishing Co.

Hart, C.H., Nelson, D.A., Robinson, C.C., Olsen, S.F., & McNeilly-Choque, M.K. (1998). Overt and relational aggression in Russian nursery-school-age children: Parenting style and marital linkages. *Developmental Psychology, 34*, 687–697.

Hirsh-Pasek, K., & Burchinal, M. (2006). Mother and caregiver sensitivity over time: Predicting language and academic outcomes with variable-and person-centered approaches. *Merrill-Palmer Quarterly, 52*(3), 449–485.

Hockenberger, E.H., Goldstein, H., & Haas, L. (1999). Commenting during joint book reading by mothers with low SES. *Topics in Early Childhood Special Education, 19*, 15–27.

Hubbs-Tait, L., Culp, A.M., Culp, R.E., & Miller, C.E. (2002). Relation of maternal cognitive stimulation, emotional support, and intrusive behavior during Head Start to children's kindergarten cognitive abilities. *Child Development, 73*(1), 110–131.

Ispa, J.M., Fine, M.A., Halgunseth, L.C., Harper, S., Robinson, J., Boyce, L., ...Brady-Smith, C. (2004). Maternal intrusiveness, maternal warmth, and mother–toddler relationship outcomes: Variations across low-income ethnic and acculturation groups. *Child Development, 75*, 1613–1631.

Kelley, S.A., Brownell, C.A., & Campbell, S.B. (2000). Mastery motivation and self-evaluative affect in toddlers: Longitudinal relations with maternal behavior. *Child Development, 71*, 1061–1071.

Kelly, J.F., Morisset, C.E., Barnard, K.E., Hammond, M.A., & Booth, C.L. (1996). The influence of early mother–child interaction on preschool cognitive/linguistic outcomes in a high-social-risk group. *Infant Mental Health Journal, 17*, 310–321.

Kim-Cohen, J., Moffitt, T.E., Caspi, A., & Taylor, A. (2004). Genetic and environmental processes in young children's resilience and vulnerability to socioeconomic deprivation. *Child Development, 75*(3), 651–668.

Laakso, M.L., Poikkeus, A.M., Eklund, K., & Lyytinen, P. (1999). Social interactional behaviors and symbolic play competence as predictors of language development and their associations with maternal attention-directing strategies. *Infant Behavior & Development, 22*, 541–556.

Landry, S.H., Smith, K.E., Miller-Loncar, C.L., & Swank, P.R. (1997). Predicting cognitive-language and social growth curves from early maternal behaviors in children at varying degrees of biological risk. *Developmental Psychology, 33*, 1040–1053.

Landry, S.H., Swank, P.R., Assel, M.A., Smith, K.E., & Vellet, S. (2001). Does early responsive parenting have a special importance for children's development or is consistency across early childhood necessary? *Developmental Psychology, 37*, 387–404.

Lee, E.J., Murry, V.M., Brody, G., & Parker, V. (2002). Maternal resources, parenting, and dietary patterns among rural African American children in single-parent families. *Public Health Nursing, 19*(2), 104–111.

Love, J.M., Kisker, E.E., Ross, C., Raikes, H., Constantine, J., Boller, K., ...Vogel, C. (2005). The effectiveness of Early Head Start for 3-year-old children and their parents: Lessons for policy and programs. *Developmental Psychology, 41*, 885–901.

MacDonald, K. (1992). Warmth as a developmental construct: An evolutionary analysis. *Child Development, 63*, 753–773.

Meins, E., Fernyhough, C. Fradley, E., & Tuckey, M. (2001). Rethinking maternal sensitivity: Mothers' comments on infants' mental processes predict security of attachment at 12 months. *Journal of Child Psychology and Psychiatry, 42*, 637–648.

Parks, S. (1997). *Hawaii Early Learning Profile (HELP)*. Palo Alto, CA: VORT Corporation.

Pederson, D.R., & Moran, G. (1995). Appendix B: Maternal Behavior Q-set. In E. Waters, B.E. Vaughn, G. Posada, & K. Kondo-Ikemura (Eds.), Caregiving, cultural, and cognitive perspectives on secure-base behavior and working models: New growing points of attachment theory and research. *Monographs of the Society for Research in Child Development, 60*(2–3, Serial No. 244), 247–254.

Peterson, C.A., Wall, S., Raikes, H.A., Kisker, E.E., Swanson, M.E., Jerald, J., ...Qiao, W. (2004). Early Head Start: Identifying and serving children with disabilities. *Topics in Early Childhood Special Education, 24*(2), 76–88.

Petrill, S.A., & Deater-Deckard, K. (2004). Task orientation, parental warmth and SES account for a significant proportion of the shared environmental variance in general cognitive ability in early childhood: Evidence from a twin study. *Developmental Science, 7*, 25–32.

Roggman, L.A., Boyce, L.K., & Innocenti, M.S. (2008). *Developmental parenting: A guide for early childhood practitioners*. Baltimore, MD: Paul H. Brookes Publishing Co.

Roggman, L.A., Cook, G.A., Innocenti, M.S., & Jump Norman, V. (2013). *The PICCOLO™ training DVD: Implementation and scoring*. Baltimore, MD: Paul H. Brookes Publishing Co.

Spencer, P.E., & Meadow-Orlans, K.P. (1996). Play, language, and maternal responsiveness: A longitudinal study of deaf and hearing infants. *Child Development, 67*, 3176–3191.

Sroufe, L.A., Egeland, B., & Kreutzer, T. (1990). The fate of early experience following developmental change: Longitudinal approaches to individual adaptation in childhood. *Child Development, 61*, 1363–1373.

Summer, G., & Spietz, A.L. (1995). *NCAST caregiver/parent–child interaction teaching manual* (2nd ed.). Seattle: University of Washington, NCAST Publications.

Tamis-LeMonda, C.S., Bornstein, M.H., & Baumwell, L. (2001). Maternal responsiveness and children's achievement of language milestones. *Child Development, 72*, 748–768.

Volker, S., Keller, H., Lohaus, A., Cappenberg, M., & Chasiotis, A. (1999). Maternal interactive behaviour in early infancy and later attachment. *International Journal of Behavioral Development, 23*, 921–936.

Wakschlag, L.S., & Hans, S.L. (1999). Relation of maternal responsiveness during infancy to the development of behavior problems in high-risk youths. *Developmental Psychology, 35*, 569–579.

Woodcock, R., & Johnson, M. (1989). *Woodcock-Johnson Psychoeducational Test Battery–Revised*. Chicago, IL: DLM.

A

Technical Report

GINA A. COOK AND LORI A. ROGGMAN

This technical report provides information on the development and psychometric properties of the observational measure *Parenting Interactions with Children: Checklist of Observations Linked to Outcomes (PICCOLO)*. PICCOLO was developed at Utah State University in Logan, Utah, with funding from the Administration for Children, Youth, and Families of the U.S. Department of Health and Human Services (Grant #90YF0500) and from a Community University Research Initiative grant from Utah State University.

After an overview of the instrument, the demographic characteristics of the samples used to develop PICCOLO are described. Then, the development of PICCOLO is discussed, including item selection, item analyses, and psychometrics. Next, descriptive statistics and information are provided about the measure's reliability, including interrater reliability and scale internal consistency. Finally, validity analyses are reported that include content validity ratings along with construct validity and predictive validity correlations.

OVERVIEW OF PICCOLO™

PICCOLO is an observational instrument to measure positive parenting. PICCOLO was developed to be easy to learn and practical to use by practitioners working with parents of young children. Psychometric data support PICCOLO as a measure that is reliable and valid. The PICCOLO domains are based on early child development theory and research suggesting critical dimensions of parent–child interactions that promote children's development in social, language, and cognitive domains. These domains include parenting behaviors indicative of affection, responsiveness, encouragement, and teaching.

Indicator items in each of these domains were observed and evaluated on more than 4,500 video-recorded observations of parents interacting with their children ages 10–47 months. The PICCOLO domain indicators describe specific interactions between parents and children at home; scoring is not determined by the presence of specific toys or materials. This distinction between observed interactions and physical toys or materials is important because in some parenting programs, materials and specific activities may be emphasized more than parent–child interactions. In PICCOLO, the focus is on what parents *do* with the materials they have and in the activities they engage in with their children.

SAMPLES FROM STUDIES PROVIDING OBSERVATION DATA

The information included in this technical report is drawn from extant observations and data from two research samples. Observations were not included if the family used a language other than English or Spanish or if the video recording was damaged, unclear, or missing. Each of these samples is described briefly next.

Early Head Start Research

Study summary: The Early Head Start (EHS) Research and Evaluation Project included 17 program sites from across the country and was funded by the Administration for Children and Families in the U.S. Department of Health and Human Services to evaluate local EHS programs serving low-income families with children from before birth to age 3 years. This program included both center-based and home-based services.

Number of programs: 17

Number of participants: 3,001

Observation procedure: Children were observed with their primary caregiver at 14, 24, and 36 months of age. The observations consisted of a 10-minute, three-bag semistructured play interaction in which the parent was presented with three bags of play materials (the first bag with a book, the second bag with pretend toys, and the third bag with other toys) and asked to play with the child for 10 minutes using the bags in numerical order, dividing the time however they wanted. Of the 3,001 families (cases) in this study, 2,287 had one or more video-recorded observations of parent–child interactions (clips); of those, 1,986 families had at least one observation coded, with a total of 4,516 clips coded.

Bilingual Early Language and Literacy Supports

Study summary: The Bilingual Early Language and Literacy Supports (BELLS) project tested language and emergent literacy outcomes of bilingual children participating in a program that serves low-income Hispanic children from birth through preschool in Utah. This program included both early English immersion and home language and literacy support.

Number of programs: 1

Number of participants: 112

Observation procedure: Children were observed with their primary caregiver at 14, 24, and 36 months of age. The observations consisted of a 15-minute two-bag play interaction (the first bag with books and the second bag with pretend toys); caregivers were asked to play with the child for 15 minutes using the bags in numerical order, dividing the time however they wanted. Of the 112 families in the sample, 62 had one or more video-recorded observations that were coded. (Attrition in this study was high due to family mobility.)

PICCOLO™ SAMPLE DESCRIPTION

Table A.1 shows the total number of families and observations from the samples described previously that were used to develop PICCOLO. These data are not intended to be nationally representative. Depending on the analytic question, either observations or families were used as the unit of analysis. The headings in the table refer to how that aspect of the sample was used in measurement development. *Reliability N* refers to the sample used to test interrater reliability across all observations scored by two or more observers. *Scale N* refers to the sample used to test scale reliability and construct validity across all observations scored by at least one observer. *Validity N* refers to the sample used to test predictive validity in cases with observations scored by at least two observers and with outcome data from children's developmental assessments at a later time point. *Descriptive N* refers to the sample used to describe the range, means, and standard deviations of PICCOLO domain and total scores at each age.

The sample from the EHS study represents low-income families of European American, African American, and Latino American ethnicities who applied for the EHS program. The sample from the BELLS study provides additional observations from low-income families of primarily Latino American ethnicity. Demographic and descriptive data reported in this section come from questionnaires completed by parents of these children.

Demographic Characteristics of Sample

The overall sample consists of 38% European American, 39% African American, and 23% Latino American families. The following tables show additional key demographic characteristics of the sample. Tables A.2 and A.3 show the proportion of family ethnicity at each level of maternal education and age.

MEASUREMENT DEVELOPMENT PROCESS

The following sections describe the methodological procedures for developing the PICCOLO measure.

Table A.1. Sample of families and observations used to develop Parenting Interactions with Children: Checklist of Observations Linked to Outcomes (PICCOLO™)

	Families		Observations	
	Validity N[a]	Descriptive N[b]	Reliability N[c]	Scale N[d]
	2+ coders	1+ coders	2+ coders	1+ coders
European American	731	788	757	1,981
African American	727	792	938	1,697
Latino American	365	468	674	920
TOTAL	1,823	2,048	2,369	4,598

[a]Validity N, number of families with at least one video observation coded by two observers and child outcome data at a later age point.

[b]Descriptive N, number of families with at least one video observation coded by at least one observer.

[c]Reliability N, number of video observations coded by at least two observers.

[d]Scale N, number of video observations coded by at least one observer.

Table A.2. Percentage of sample by maternal education within each ethnicity

Education	European American (%)	African American (%)	Latino American (%)	Total (%)
Less than HS	31	48	65	45
HS or GED	39	29	20	31
HS + additional education	30	23	14	24

Key: GED, obtained general equivalency diploma; HS, completed high school.

Table A.3. Percentage of sample by maternal age within each ethnicity

Age	European American (%)	African American (%)	Latino American (%)	Total (%)
Teen mother	32	53	31	39
$\geq$ 20 years old	68	48	69	61

Item Development

PICCOLO items were developed and identified initially by examining several sources. First, we examined definitions of constructs indicated in the research literature as linked to child outcomes and constructs central to major theories of child development. Second, we examined definitions of constructs we have found in our previous research to be linked to child outcomes in Head Start, EHS, and other low-income populations. Third, we examined other existing observational measures of parent–child interaction, such as instruments widely used in the research literature. These instruments included Home Observation for Measurement of the Environment (HOME; Caldwell & Bradley, 1984); NCAST (Barnard & Kelly, 1990; Summer & Spietz, 1995); Maternal Behavior Q-set (Pederson & Moran, 1995); and assessment tools used by our Head Start program partners, such as the indicators described as interactive behaviors in the Hawaii Early Learning Profile (HELP; Parks, 1997), to identify behavioral indicators of positive parent–child interaction. Measures used for this purpose have established psychometric properties and are appropriate for low-income families from culturally and linguistically diverse groups. Finally, we reviewed with our Head Start program partners their program documentation, stated objectives, and intended outcomes for parent–child relationships. We used these program materials to identify additional potential behavioral indicators that would be important for these and similar programs.

All possible items were reviewed, and redundant items were combined or eliminated. Approximately 200 item "candidates" were evaluated by the research team and by additional colleagues for clarity and relevance to parent–child relationships and children's developmental outcomes. Any items describing abstract or complex aspects of parenting or parent–child interaction were not included unless they could be reworded to be concrete and parsimonious without losing their meaning. Items that could not be clarified in this way were eliminated. The remaining 112 items were selected for further work.

The clarity and usefulness of behavioral indicators ultimately rests with those who use them to assess parent–child interaction. After initially reviewing various sources described previously for appropriate items and clarifying the wording of items to make them as clear and concrete as possible, we received feedback from untrained observers about both the clarity and importance of each item. Some behaviors, even if clear and valued in the research literature, were neither clear nor important to nonresearchers.

EHS staff and parent volunteers ($n = 9$) were asked to rate the large set of identified and reworded items in two ways. *How clearly is the item defined*—Would you recognize the behavior if you saw it? *How important is the item*—How essential is it for children's development? These ratings were used to identify items that needed to be clarified and to reduce the number of items to be tested in the initial version of the measure. To ensure that items are useful and appropriate for Spanish-speaking families, items were professionally translated into Spanish (with back translation) and then evaluated separately by a group of Spanish-speaking staff and parent volunteers ($n = 4$).

After considering these ratings and reviews, 80 items were selected for testing through observations of archived video-recorded observations of parent–child interaction.

Item Selection

Teams of independent coders, recruited from undergraduate students in child development and psychology classes at Utah State University, tested the initial version of our checklist measure by coding observations from our video archive. Each student received 8–10 hours of training before observing video clips. Training included reading basic information about confidentiality protections, observational procedures, and parent–child interaction dimensions. To ensure that students understood the material they had read, each student was given a short quiz on the readings, and all students correctly answered at least 80% of the items before they were allowed to proceed. After training and certification in confidentiality procedures, students observed example video clips in small groups and discussed the observations with a member of the research team until reaching consensus. After passing a reliability test, students were assigned to code video clips. For assessing item reliability, two or more coders observed each video-recorded observation. For assessing predictive validity, at least two reliable coders observed each video-recorded observation.

Multiple criteria were used to select the final PICCOLO items based on 1) variability across individual cases, 2) reliability of raters, 3) scale reliability within domains, 4) construct validity with extant parenting measures, 5) predictive validity with extant child outcome data, 6) content validity from the importance ratings from program partners, and 7) qualitative feedback from raters and partners. Variability is shown in Table A.4.

RELIABILITY

Reliability refers to the degree to which the instrument is free from random error associated with the process of measuring the construct of interest. One step in minimizing random error in PICCOLO involves training materials that provide potential observers with a clear and comprehensive understanding of the instrument's purposes and procedures.

Training Observers

As part of the PICCOLO training, trainees read about the content and purpose of the measure (3 hours) and then watched and discussed five 10-minute video-

Table A.4. Descriptive statistics on Parenting Interactions with Children: Checklist of Observations Linked to Outcomes (PICCOLO™) at child age 14 months (*n* = 1,587), 24 months (*n* = 1,504), and 36 months (*n* = 1,401)

Descriptive statistics	Minimum	Maximum	Mean total score	Total score standard deviation
Affection				
14 months	1.17	14.00	10.91	2.01
24 months	2.50	14.00	10.75	2.09
36 months	1.00	14.00	10.45	2.07
Responsiveness				
14 months	0.00	14.00	10.63	2.16
24 months	1.75	14.00	11.27	2.06
36 months	1.40	14.00	11.29	2.06
Encouragement				
14 months	1.00	14.00	9.65	2.36
24 months	1.00	14.00	10.36	2.32
36 months	0.00	14.00	10.19	2.30
Teaching				
14 months	0.00	16.00	7.35	2.79
24 months	0.00	16.00	8.70	2.83
36 months	0.00	16.00	8.61	2.79
PICCOLO total				
14 months	7.48	58.00	38.53	7.66
24 months	12.26	58.00	41.09	7.77
36 months	6.09	58.00	40.54	7.68

Note: Statistics are based on descriptive sample of 2,048 families, with any scores by multiple coders averaged together; data from child age 10 months not included.

recorded segments previously observed by at least three expert observers who coded by consensus (3 hours). The consensus ratings established a standard by which to judge the accuracy of ratings made by trainees, and ratings that were not in agreement were then used to pinpoint additional training needs. At the end of training, potential users took a reliability test in which they watched and coded three to five additional 10-minute video-recorded observations to reach a level of 80% agreement with research team ratings (2–4 hours).

Interrater Reliability

To assess interrater reliability of the PICCOLO items, independently coded video-recorded observations were compared between two observers. The mean proportion of absolute agreement across observations is shown for each PICCOLO item and domain in Tables A.5–A.8. The mean interrater correlation is shown for each domain and the total score in Table A.9.

Interrater Reliability by Ethnicity

To assess cross-cultural reliability of the PICCOLO items, independently coded video-recorded observations were compared between observers of different ethnicities.

Table A.5. Domain 1: Affection

Item	Average interrater agreement
1. Speaks in a warm tone of voice	0.89
2. Smiles at child	0.68
3. Praises child	0.70
4. Is physically close to child	0.95
5. Uses positive expressions with child	0.73
6. Is engaged in interacting with child	0.87
7. Shows emotional warmth	0.69
Total = 7 items	**0.80**

Table A.6. Domain 2: Responsiveness

Item	Average interrater agreement
1. Pays attention to what child is doing	0.92
2. Changes pace or activity to meet child's interests or needs	0.67
3. Is flexible about child's change of activities or interests	0.78
4. Follows what child is trying to do	0.73
5. Responds to child's emotions	0.64
6. Looks at child when child talks or makes sounds	0.76
7. Replies to child's words or sounds	0.78
Total = 7 items	**0.76**

Table A.7. Domain 3: Encouragement

Item	Average interrater agreement
1. Waits for child's response after making a suggestion	0.61
2. Encourages child to handle toys	0.90
3. Supports child in making choices	0.72
4. Supports child in doing things on his or her own	0.82
5. Verbally encourages child's efforts	0.67
6. Offers suggestions to help child	0.67
7. Shows enthusiasm about what child is doing	0.70
Total = 7 items	**0.73**

Table A.8. Domain 4: Teaching

Item	Average interrater agreement
1. Explains reasons for something to child	0.76
2. Suggests activities to extend what child is doing	0.61
3. Repeats or expands child's words or sounds	0.67
4. Labels objects or actions for child	0.74
5. Engages in pretend play with child	0.66
6. Does activities in a sequence of steps	0.71
7. Talks to child about characteristics of objects	0.69
8. Asks child for information	0.68
Total = 8 items	**0.69**

Table A.9. Interrater reliability correlations

Domain	Reliability with another coder
Affection	.80
Responsiveness	.74
Encouragement	.77
Teaching	.76
PICCOLO Total	**.77**

Key: PICCOLO™, Parenting Interactions with Children: Checklist of Observations Linked to Outcomes.

Each video clip was originally coded by a coder of the same ethnicity as that of the parent. Coders included European Americans, African Americans, and Latinos. Spanish-speaking families were observed by native Spanish-speaking coders. More than 500 observations were coded by two or more observers from a culture different from that of the parent and the original coder. The mean proportion of agreement by culture is shown for each domain in Table A.10.

Table A.10. Cross-ethnicity reliability correlations by domain

Domain	Coder ethnicity	Reliability with coders of another ethnicity
Affection		**.78**
	European American	.82
	African American	.76
	Latino	.75
Responsiveness		**.68**
	European American	.73
	African American	.64
	Latino	.67
Encouragement		**.66**
	European American	.72
	African American	.60
	Latino	.67
Teaching		**.75**
	European American	.79
	African American	.73
	Latino	.72
PICCOLO Total		**.80**
	European American	.81
	African American	.82
	Latino	.76

Key: PICCOLO™, Parenting Interactions with Children: Checklist of Observations Linked to Outcomes.

Scale Reliability

PICCOLO was developed using a theoretical framework suggesting four major domains of parenting behaviors: Affection (warmth, care), Responsiveness (sensitivity), Encouragement (scaffolding, autonomy support), and Teaching (cognitive stimulation, language and literacy support). To test the degree to which data from actual parent–child interactions matched this theoretical framework, we conducted both internal consistency and confirmatory factor analyses on the data. Tables A.11–A.14 show the item descriptions and internal consistency statistics for items within each domain. Table A.15 presents the results of the confirmatory factor analyses. Within each domain, factor loadings are in the moderate to high range, consistent with internal consistency within each domain. Given the factor loadings, the internal

Table A.11.   Internal consistency of the Affection domain (scale *alpha* = .78)

Item	Corrected item–total correlation	Cronbach's *alpha* if item deleted
1. Speaks in a warm tone of voice	.57	.75
2. Smiles at child	.54	.76
3. Praises child	.42	.79
4. Is physically close to child	.29	.79
5. Uses positive expressions with child	.75	.70
6. Is engaged in interacting with child	.55	.75
7. Shows emotional warmth	.63	.73

Table A.12.   Internal consistency of the Responsiveness domain (scale *alpha* = .75)

Item	Corrected item–total correlation	Cronbach's *alpha* if item deleted
1. Pays attention to what child is doing	.45	.73
2. Changes pace or activity to meet child's interests or needs	.45	.72
3. Is flexible about child's change of activities or interests	.49	.71
4. Follows what child is trying to do	.60	.68
5. Responds to child's emotions	.47	.71
6. Looks at child when child talks or makes sounds	.45	.72
7. Replies to child's words or sounds	.41	.73

Table A.13.   Internal consistency of the Encouragement domain (scale *alpha* = .77)

Item	Corrected item–total correlation	Cronbach's *alpha* if item deleted
1. Waits for child's response after making a suggestion	.49	.74
2. Encourages child to handle toys	.46	.75
3. Supports child in making choices	.49	.74
4. Supports child in doing things on his or her own	.45	.75
5. Verbally encourages child's efforts	.52	.73
6. Offers suggestions to help child	.50	.74
7. Shows enthusiasm about what child is doing	.57	.72

Table A.14. Internal consistency of the Teaching domain (scale *alpha* = .80)

Item	Corrected item–total correlation	Cronbach's *alpha* if item deleted
1. Explains reasons for something to child	.53	.77
2. Suggests activities to extend what child is doing	.55	.77
3. Repeats or expands child's words or sounds	.45	.78
4. Labels objects or actions for child	.53	.77
5. Engages in pretend play with child	.48	.78
6. Does activities in a sequence of steps	.52	.77
7. Talks to child about characteristics of objects	.48	.78
8. Asks child for information	.51	.77

Table A.15. Confirmatory factor analysis results for single factor in each domain

Items in each domain	Factor loadings
Affection	
1. Speaks in a warm tone of voice	.74
2. Smiles at child	.67
3. Praises child	.54
4. Is physically close to child	.43
5. Uses positive expressions with child	.86
6. Is engaged in interacting with child	.71
7. Shows emotional warmth	.78
Responsiveness	
1. Pays attention to what child is doing	.62
2. Changes pace or activity to meet child's interests or needs	.64
3. Is flexible about child's change of activities or interests	.67
4. Follows what child is trying to do	.78
5. Responds to child's emotions	.64
6. Looks at child when child talks or makes sounds	.58
7. Replies to child's words or sounds	.55
Encouragement	
1. Waits for child's response after making a suggestion	.65
2. Encourages child to handle toys	.64
3. Supports child in making choices	.68
4. Supports child in doing things on his or her own	.64
5. Verbally encourages child's efforts	.65
6. Offers suggestions to help child	.62
7. Shows enthusiasm about what child is doing	.70
Teaching	
1. Explains reasons for something to child	.67
2. Suggests activities to extend what child is doing	.69
3. Repeats or expands child's words or sounds	.58
4. Labels objects or actions for child	.67
5. Engages in pretend play with child	.62
6. Does activities in a sequence of steps	.66
7. Talks to child about characteristics of objects	.62
8. Asks child for information	.65

Table A.16. Correlations among domains at 14 months ($n = 1,587$)

Domain	Affection	Responsiveness	Encouragement	Teaching
Affection	1.00	—	—	—
Responsiveness	.61	1.00	—	—
Encouragement	.73	.68	1.00	—
Teaching	.53	.35	.57	1.00

Note: All correlations are significant at $p < .001$.

Table A.17. Correlations among domains at 24 months ($n = 1,504$)

Domain	Affection	Responsiveness	Encouragement	Teaching
Affection	1.00	—	—	—
Responsiveness	.65	1.00	—	—
Encouragement	.72	.72	1.00	—
Teaching	.54	.44	.57	1.00

Note: All correlations are significant at $p < .001$.

Table A.18. Correlations among domains at 36 months ($n = 1,401$)

Domain	Affection	Responsiveness	Encouragement	Teaching
Affection	1.00	—	—	—
Responsiveness	.65	1.00	—	—
Encouragement	.71	.72	1.00	—
Teaching	.53	.43	.57	1.00

Note: All correlations are significant at $p < .001$.

consistency within all four domains, and the strong theoretical basis of each of these domains, we recommend the use of all four domains. As shown in Tables A.16–A.18, PICCOLO domains are moderately to highly correlated with one another, although less so over time and not at a level that would suggest that they measure the same construct.

Scale Stability

Another aspect of scale reliability is stability over time. As displayed in Tables A.19–A.22, the PICCOLO domains are moderately stable over time in that earlier scores predict later scores in the same domain. There are, nevertheless, changes over time in some domains. Tables A.23 and A.24 show *t*-test results from comparisons of

Table A.19. Stability correlations for the Affection domain ($n = 1,055–1,174$)

Age	14 months	24 months
14 months	1.00	—
24 months	.49	1.00
36 months	.39	.49

Note: All correlations significant at $p < .001$.

Table A.20. Stability correlations for the Responsiveness domain ($n = 1{,}054$–$1{,}176$)

Age	14 months	24 months
14 months	1.00	—
24 months	.40	1.00
36 months	.30	.39

Note: All correlations are significant at $p < .001$.

Table A.21. Stability correlations for the Encouragement domain ($n = 1{,}055$–$1{,}174$)

Age	14 months	24 months
14 months	1.00	—
24 months	.44	1.00
36 months	.36	.46

Note: All correlations are significant at $p < .001$.

Table A.22. Stability correlations for the Teaching domain ($n = 1{,}055$–$1{,}176$)

Age	14 months	24 months
14 months	1.00	—
24 months	.52	1.00
36 months	.41	.52

Note: All correlations are significant at $p < .001$.

Table A.23. Paired samples t-tests testing changes in scores between 14 and 24 months

Domain and child age	Item mean	N	Standard deviation	Standard error of the mean	t	Significance (2-tailed)
Affection 14 months	1.57	1,174	.28	.01	—	—
Affection 24 months	1.54	1,174	.30	.01	3.89	.00
Responsiveness 14 months	1.53	1,176	.31	.01	—	—
Responsiveness 24 months	1.61	1,176	.30	.01	−8.72	.00
Encouragement 14 months	1.39	1,174	.33	.01	—	—
Encouragement 24 months	1.49	1,174	.33	.01	−9.32	.00
Teaching 14 months	.93	1,176	.35	.01	—	—
Teaching 24 months	1.09	1,176	.36	.01	−15.34	.00

Note: Mean values are only for cases with video observations at both time points.

domain scores between adjacent time points, with most changes occurring between 14 and 24 months.

VALIDITY

Several aspects of validity were examined both to guide item selection and to assess the psychometric strength of the final measure. Validity concerns included *content*

Table A.24. Paired samples *t*-tests testing changes in scores between 24 and 36 months

Domain and child age	Item mean	N	Standard deviation	Standard error of the mean	t	Significance (2-tailed)
Affection 24 months	1.54	1,104	.30	.01	—	—
Affection 36 months	1.50	1,104	.30	.01	4.42	.00
Responsiveness 24 months	1.62	1,103	.29	.01	—	—
Responsiveness 36 months	1.61	1,103	.30	.01	0.25	.81
Encouragement 24 months	1.48	1,104	.33	.01	—	—
Encouragement 36 months	1.46	1,104	.33	.01	2.25	.03
Teaching 24 months	1.09	1,104	.36	.01	—	—
Teaching 36 months	1.08	1,104	.35	.01	0.67	.50

Note: Mean values are only for cases with video observations at both time points.

validity, the extent to which practitioners in the field perceived the measure as including items that were important for parenting; *construct validity,* the relations between the PICCOLO measure and an established observational measure of parenting; and *predictive validity,* the association of the PICCOLO measure with positive child outcomes. The following aspects of validity were examined:

- Content validity from importance ratings by practitioners

- Construct validity in relation to established observational measure of parenting

- Predictive validity in relation to measures of child outcomes

Content Validity

PICCOLO was developed based on an extensive literature review of parent–child interactions related to children's later cognitive and social development. The domains were developed from a review of items from observational instruments used in previous parenting research. Throughout this process, numerous experts in parent–child interactions have agreed that PICCOLO measures aspects of parenting that are important in determining child outcomes, suggesting considerable content validity.

The usefulness of PICCOLO for program staff was evaluated using trained practitioners in two home-based EHS programs and one other home visiting program. Practitioners used the measure and gave feedback on ease of use, meaningfulness, and appropriateness of the measure. Practitioners rated each item in terms of its importance in parenting, using a 0–3 scale with 0 = *not at all important,* 1 = *somewhat important,* 2 = *fairly important,* and 3 = *very important.* The average importance rating for the selected PICCOLO items was 2.6 versus 2.3 for those items that were eliminated. Tables A.25–A.28 show the importance ratings for items in each domain.

Construct Validity

Construct validity assesses the extent to which a measure is associated empirically with other measures of similar constructs. In the EHS Research and Evaluation Project, an established reliable and valid observational parenting measure (Berlin,

Table A.25. Affection domain: Content validity ratings

Descriptive statistics	Minimum	Maximum	Mean	Standard deviation
1. Speaks in a warm tone of voice	2.00	3.00	2.56	0.53
2. Smiles at child	1.00	3.00	2.44	0.73
3. Praises child	2.00	3.00	2.67	0.50
4. Is physically close to child	1.00	3.00	2.56	0.73
5. Uses positive expressions with child	2.00	3.00	2.89	0.33
6. Is engaged in interacting with child	3.00	3.00	3.00	0.00
7. Shows emotional warmth	3.00	3.00	3.00	0.00

Table A.26. Responsiveness domain: Content validity ratings

Descriptive statistics	Minimum	Maximum	Mean	Standard deviation
1. Pays attention to what child is doing	0.00	3.00	2.00	1.20
2. Changes pace or activity to meet child's interests or needs	2.00	3.00	2.50	0.53
3. Is flexible about child's change of activities or interests	2.00	3.00	2.75	0.46
4. Follows what child is trying to do	2.00	3.00	2.88	0.35
5. Responds to child's emotions	1.00	3.00	2.50	0.76
6. Looks at child when child talks or makes sounds	2.00	3.00	2.88	0.35
7. Replies to child's words or sounds	2.00	3.00	2.88	0.35

Table A.27. Encouragement domain: Content validity ratings

Descriptive statistics	Minimum	Maximum	Mean	Standard deviation
1. Waits for child's response after making a suggestion	2.00	3.00	2.78	0.44
2. Encourages child to handle toys	2.00	3.00	2.89	0.33
3. Supports child in making choices	2.00	3.00	2.89	0.33
4. Supports child in doing things on his or her own	1.00	3.00	2.56	0.73
5. Verbally encourages child's efforts	2.00	3.00	2.89	0.33
6. Offers suggestions to help child	1.00	3.00	2.00	0.50
7. Shows enthusiasm about what child is doing	2.00	3.00	2.44	0.53

Table A.28. Teaching domain: Content validity ratings

Descriptive statistics	Minimum	Maximum	Mean	Standard deviation
1. Explains reasons for something to child	1.00	3.00	2.13	0.83
2. Suggests activities to extend what child is doing	1.00	3.00	2.13	0.83
3. Repeats or expands child's words or sounds	2.00	3.00	2.75	0.46
4. Labels objects or actions for child	1.00	3.00	2.38	0.92
5. Engages in pretend play with child	3.00	3.00	3.00	0.00
6. Does activities in a sequence of steps	2.00	3.00	2.38	0.52
7. Talks to child about characteristics of objects	1.00	3.00	1.75	0.71
8. Asks child for information	1.00	3.00	2.25	0.89

Brady-Smith, & Brooks-Gunn, 2002; Fuligni & Brooks-Gunn, 2013) was used by a team of research scholars at Columbia University to code the same semistructured observations used for the development of PICCOLO. The dimensions of positive parenting in the established measure included Sensitivity, Cognitive Stimulation, and Positive Regard. *Sensitivity* was defined as the degree to which the parent was sensitive and child focused, provided praise and encouragement, and established a balance between giving support and allowing independent exploration. *Cognitive Stimulation* was defined as parent efforts to enhance perceptual, cognitive, and language development; to show awareness of the child's developmental level; and to make efforts to bring the child above that level. *Positive Regard* was defined as the parent's expressions of love, respect, and/or admiration for the child, including the quality and quantity of behaviors such as hugging, smiling, praising, and showing clear enjoyment of child. These three ratings were intercorrelated ($r = .59$–62; Berlin et al., 2002) and combined into one scale of Supportiveness for the national study (*alpha* = .82; Berlin et al., 2002) but were also used separately to examine the construct validity of specific PICCOLO domains. Reliability of the ratings was established at 85% agreement and maintained at 90%, allowing 1-point difference in scores (Administration for Children and Families, 2002).

To examine the construct validity of PICCOLO, ratings of Sensitivity, Cognitive Stimulation, and Positive Regard were examined in relation to the PICCOLO domains of Responsiveness, Teaching, and Affection, respectively. The PICCOLO domain of Encouragement was also examined in relation to these dimensions of positive parenting available from the same observations but did not consistently overlap in definition with one of them. Encouragement and the PICCOLO total score were also examined in relation to the Supportiveness scale. Tables A.29–A.31 show the associations at three age points between PICCOLO and the measure used to code the same observations in the EHS Research and Evaluation Project. Correlations are shown for European Americans, African Americans, and Latino Americans.

Predictive Validity

PICCOLO was designed to assess parenting behaviors that are directly associated with children's positive outcomes, particularly the known indicators of school readiness. In this study, PICCOLO items and domains were significantly correlated with positive child outcomes within each ethnic group and across all three ethnic groups combined.

All four domains were predictive of child development outcomes. When PICCOLO scores were high in any of the domains, children's assessment scores were generally higher on measures of their cognitive and language development and often their social-emotional development as well. Table A.32 shows PICCOLO total and domain scores in relation to specific child outcomes for the combined sample and separate ethnic groups.

To test the overall predictive validity of the PICCOLO scores, summary outcome variables were calculated using z-scores from outcome measures: a cognitive-language outcome variable (Peabody Picture Vocabulary Test–Third Edition [PPVT; Dunn & Dunn, 1997] and Bayley Scales of Infant Development: Mental Development Index [Bayley, 1993] at age 3, *alpha* = .72; PPVT and Woodcock-Johnson Psycho-educational Test Battery–Revised: Letter Word and Applied Problems [Woodcock

Table A.29. Construct validity at 14 months for total sample, European Americans (EA), African Americans (AA), and Latino Americans (LA)

Domains	Sensitivity				Cognitive Stimulation				Positive Regard				Supportiveness			
	Total	EA	AA	LA	Total	EA	AA	LA	Total	EA	AA	LA	Total	EA	AA	LA
Affection	.43	.41	.45	.41	.45	.44	.42	.44	.55	.53	.56	.56	.55	.53	.56	.57
Responsiveness	.39	.41	.44	.31	.29	.27	.30	.24	.32	.31	.36	.25	.39	.39	.44	.31
Encouragement	.43	.44	.47	.33	.41	.41	.43	.32	.44	.42	.48	.38	.50	.49	.55	.41
Teaching	.31	.32	.40	.27	.56	.52	.63	.52	.38	.35	.47	.37	.48	.47	.58	.46
PICCOLO total	.47	.48	.53	.39	.53	.51	.56	.46	.51	.49	.57	.47	.58	.57	.65	.52

Note: Total sample ($N = 1{,}458$–$1{,}575$); European American ($n = 625$–660); African American ($n = 568$–623); Latino American ($n = 266$–292). For all correlations, $p < .001$.

Key: PICCOLO™, Parenting Interactions with Children: Checklist of Observations Linked to Outcomes.

Table A.30. Construct validity at 24 months for total sample, European Americans (EA), African Americans (AA), and Latino Americans (LA)

Domains	Sensitivity				Cognitive Stimulation				Positive Regard				Supportiveness			
	Total	EA	AA	LA	Total	EA	AA	LA	Total	EA	AA	LA	Total	EA	AA	LA
Affection	.50	.42	.59	.39	.50	.40	.49	.32	.54	.46	.60	.52	.57	.50	.41	.50
Responsiveness	.42	.33	.50	.36	.33	.26	.38	.29	.35	.25	.40	.37	.42	.32	.49	.41
Encouragement	.47	.37	.57	.28	.39	.34	.47	.21	.42	.30	.48	.37	.49	.39	.59	.35
Teaching	.40	.34	.52	.35	.56	.50	.66	.55	.36	.30	.41	.35	.51	.44	.41	.52
PICCOLO total	.49	.40	.55	.48	.52	.48	.60	.43	.54	.46	.60	.52	.60	.51	.69	.53

Note: Total sample (*N* = 1449); European American (*n* = 614); African American (*n* = 555); Latino American (*n* = 280). For all correlations, *p* < .001.

Key: PICCOLO™, Parenting Interactions with Children: Checklist of Observations Linked to Outcomes.

Table A.31. Construct validity at 36 months for total sample, European Americans (EA), African Americans (AA), and Latino Americans (LA)

Domains	Sensitivity				Cognitive Stimulation				Positive Regard				Supportiveness			
	Total	EA	AA	LA	Total	EA	AA	LA	Total	EA	AA	LA	Total	EA	AA	LA
Affection	.49	.39	.58	.47	.38	.27	.47	.41	.57	.47	.65	.60	.55	.44	.34	.57
Responsiveness	.40	.27	.50	.41	.26	.13	.35	.33	.34	.23	.41	.39	.38	.24	.48	.44
Encouragement	.43	.37	.49	.35	.30	.25	.36	.29	.41	.34	.45	.41	.44	.38	.50	.41
Teaching	.36	.29	.43	.43	.51	.41	.63	.57	.35	.27	.39	.43	.48	.38	.38	.58
PICCOLO total	.50	.40	.59	.48	.44	.34	.55	.48	.50	.39	.56	.55	.56	.44	.65	.59

Note: Total sample (*N* = 1,328–1,332); European American (*n* = 558–560); African American (*n* = 558–560); European American (*n* = 397–398); Latino American (*n* = 265–266). For all correlations, *p* < .001.

Key: PICCOLO™, Parenting Interactions with Children: Checklist of Observations Linked to Outcomes.

Table A.32. Predictive validity correlations for domains and total scores at each age with later child development outcomes

Domains and ages	Total sample (N = 880–1,261)	European American (n = 385–544)	Latino American (n = 102–222)	African American (n = 313–495)
Affection				
14 months	.27**** MDI 24 .24**** MDI 36 .17**** CDI 24[a] .12**** BRS 24 .22**** PPVT 36[a] .26**** PPVT PK[a] .17**** WJLW PK[a] .19**** WJAP PK[a]	.18**** MDI 24 .20**** MDI 36 .18**** PPVT 36 .17**** PPVT PK .18**** WJLW PK .16**** WJAP PK	.26**** MDI 24 .13* CDI 24[a] .15* BRS 24 .15* BRS 36 .24**** PPVT 36[a] .17* PPVT PK .13* WJAP PK[a]	.18**** MDI 24 .19**** MDI 36 .12** BRS 24 .21**** PPVT 36 .23**** PPVT PK .20**** WJAP PK
24 months	.28**** MDI 36 .25**** PPVT 36[a] .30**** PPVT PK[a] .18**** WJLW PK[a] .21**** WJAP PK[a]	.23**** MDI 36 –.16**** CBC PK .16*** PPVT 36 .16**** PPVT PK	.21*** PPVT 36[a] .26*** PPVT PK .13* WJAP PK[a]	.17**** MDI 36 .14*** PPVT 36 .22**** PPVT PK .23**** WJLW PK .21**** WJAP PK
36 months	.27**** PPVT PK[a] .22**** WJLW PK[a] .16**** WJAP PK[a]	.16**** PPVT PK .21**** WJLW PK	.38**** PPVT PK	.20**** PPVT PK .21**** WJLW PK .16*** WJAP PK
Responsiveness				
14 months	.19**** MDI 24 .18**** MDI 36 .16**** CDI 24[a] .16**** PPVT 36[a] .21**** PPVT PK[a] .15**** WJLW PK[a] .16**** WJAP PK[a]	.22**** MDI 24 .25**** MDI 36 .14**** CDI 24 .15*** PPVT 36 .19**** PPVT PK .18**** WJLW PK .15*** WJAP PK	.20*** MDI 24 .20*** CDI 24[a] .14** WJLW PK[a]	.15*** MDI 24 .17**** CDI 24 .14*** BRS 24 .20**** PPVT 36 .20**** PPVT PK .13* WJLW PK .19**** WJAP PK
24 months	.23**** MDI 36 .22**** PPVT 36[a] .24**** PPVT PK[a] .15**** WJLW PK[a] .19**** WJAP PK[a]	.27**** MDI 36 .19**** PPVT 36 .21**** PPVT PK .18**** WJLW PK .14*** WJAP PK	.17* MDI 36 .18** PPVT 36[a] .19* PPVT PK .13* WJLW PK[a] .14* WJAP PK[a]	.18**** MDI 36 –.16**** CBC 36 .27**** PPVT 36 .25**** PPVT PK .26**** WJLW PK .23**** WJAP PK
36 months	.22**** PPVT PK[a] .16**** WJLW PK[a] .13**** WJAP PK[a]	–.15**** CBC PK .20**** PPVT PK .18**** WJLW PK .13*** WJAP PK	.24* PPVT PK	.25**** PPVT PK .17**** WJLW PK .18**** WJAP PK
Encouragement				
14 months	.24**** MDI 24 .23**** MDI 36 .13**** CDI 24[a] .19**** PPVT 36[a] .23**** PPVT PK[a] .15**** WJLW PK[a] .16**** WJAP PK[a]	.21**** MDI 24 .26**** MDI 36 .12*** CDI 24 .20**** PPVT 36 .21**** PPVT PK .19**** WJLW PK .14*** WJAP PK	.24**** MDI 24 .12* CDI 24[a] .19** BRS 24 .19** BRS 36 .15* PPVT 36[a]	.25**** MDI 24 .23**** MDI 36 .15**** CDI 24 .15*** BRS 24 .28**** PPVT 36 .25**** PPVT PK .13* WJLW PK .22**** WJAP PK
24 months	.24**** MDI 36 .24**** PPVT 36[a] .28**** PPVT PK[a] .14**** WJLW PK[a] .20**** WJAP PK[a]	.24**** MDI 36 –.13*** CBC PK .25**** PPVT 36 .21**** PPVT PK .13*** WJAP PK	.22**** BRS 36 .19** PPVT 36[a]	.19**** MDI 36 –.13*** CBC 36 .27**** PPVT 36 .23**** PPVT PK .26**** N = 322 WJLW PK .25**** N = 424 WJAP PK
36 months	.24**** PPVT PK[a] .21**** WJLW PK[a] .17**** WJAP PK[a]	.17**** PPVT PK .24**** WJLW PK .15**** WJAP PK	–.16* CBC PK	.21**** PPVT PK .24**** WJLW PK .19**** WJAP PK

(continued)

Table A.32. *(continued)*

Domains and ages	Total sample ($N = 880–1,261$)	European American ($n = 385–544$)	Latino American ($n = 102–222$)	African American ($n = 313–495$)
Teaching				
14 months	.22**** MDI 24 .18**** MDI 36 .13 **** CDI 24[a] .20**** PPVT 36[a] .20**** PPVT PK[a] .15**** WJLW PK[a] .13**** WJAP PK[a]	.21**** MDI 24 .22**** MDI 36 .13*** CDI 24 .26**** PPVT 36 .17**** PPVT PK .12* WJLW PK	.23**** MDI 24 .18** BRS 24 .28**** BRS 36 .18** PPVT 36[a] .18* PPVT PK .14* WJAP PK[a]	.27**** MDI 24 .25**** MDI 36 .17**** CDI 24 .16**** BRS 24 .22**** PPVT 36 .29**** PPVT PK .21**** WJLW PK .18**** WJAP PK
24 months	.24**** MDI 36 .20**** PPVT 36[a] .24**** PPVT PK[a] .18**** WJLW PK[a] .16**** WJAP PK[a]	.27**** MDI 36 −.18**** CBC PK .19**** PPVT 36 .20**** PPVT PK .16*** WJLW PK .12** WJAP PK	.18** MDI 36 .16* BRS 36 .24**** PPVT 36[a] .33**** PPVT PK .14* WJLW PK[a] .15** WJAP PK[a]	.25**** MDI 36 −.12** CBC 36 .26**** PPVT 36 .23**** PPVT PK .22**** WJLW PK .22**** WJAP PK
36 months	.24**** PPVT PK[a] .22**** WJLW PK[a] .15**** WJAP PK[a]	.22**** PPVT PK .21**** WJLW PK .17**** WJAP PK	.30*** PPVT PK .17** WJLW PK[a]	.31**** PPVT PK .27**** WJLW PK .21**** WJAP PK
PICCOLO total				
14 months	.23**** MDI 24 .19**** MDI 36 .13 **** CDI 24[a] .24**** PPVT 36[a] .21**** PPVT PK[a] .15**** WJLW PK[a] .14**** WJAP PK[a]	.21**** MDI 24 .22**** MDI 36 .13*** CDI 24 .26**** PPVT 36 .17**** PPVT PK .12* WJLW PK	.23**** MDI 24 .18** BRS 24 .28**** BRS 36 .18** PPVT 36[a] .18* PPVT PK .14* WJAP PK[a]	.27**** MDI 24 .25**** MDI 36 .17**** CDI 24 .16**** BRS 24 .22**** PPVT 36 .29**** PPVT PK .21**** WJLW PK .18**** WJAP PK
24 months	.25**** MDI 36 .24**** PPVT 36[a] .23**** PPVT PK[a] .19**** WJLW PK[a] .16**** WJAP PK[a]	.27**** MDI 36 −.18**** CBC PK .19**** PPVT 36 .20**** PPVT PK .16*** WJLW PK .12** WJAP PK	.18** MDI 36 .16* BRS 36 .24**** PPVT 36[a] .33**** PPVT PK .14* WJLW PK[a] .15** WJAP PK[a]	.25**** MDI 36 −.12** CBC 36 .26**** PPVT 36 .23**** PPVT PK .22**** WJLW PK .22**** WJAP PK
36 months	.25**** PPVT PK[a] .24**** WJLW PK[a] .16**** WJAP PK[a]	.22**** PPVT PK .21**** WJLW PK .17**** WJAP PK	.30*** PPVT PK .17** WJLW PK[a]	.31**** PPVT PK .27**** WJLW PK .21**** WJAP PK

Note: Correlations are included in the table if $p < .05$ and $r > .11$.

Key: BRS, Bayley Scales of Infant Development: Behavior Rating Scales: Emotion Regulation (24 months, 36 months; Bayley, 1993); CBC, Child Behavior Checklist Aggression score (24 months, 36 months; Achenbach & Rescorla, 2000); CDI, Communication Development Index: Vocabulary Production (24 months; Fenson et al., 1994); MDI, Bayley Scales of Infant Development: Mental Development Index: Cognitive Development (24 months, 36 months; Bayley, 1993); PPVT, Peabody Picture Vocabulary Test–Third Edition: Receptive Vocabulary (36 months, prekindergarten; Dunn & Dunn, 1997); WJAP, Woodcock-Johnson Psychoeducational Test Battery–Revised: Applied Problems: Problem Solving (prekindergarten; Woodcock & Johnson, 1989); WJLW, Woodcock-Johnson Psychoeducational Test Battery–Revised: Letter Word: Emergent Literacy (prekindergarten; Woodcock & Johnson, 1989); 24, 24 months; 36, 36 months; PK, prekindergarten.

* $p < .05$; ** $p < .01$; *** $p < .001$; **** $p < .0001$.

[a]Partial correlation controlling for test language (English or Spanish).

& Johnson, 1989] at prekindergarten, *alpha* = .74) and a cognitive-language-social outcome variable (adding Bayley Scales of Infant Development: Behavior Rating Scales [Bayley, 1993] and reverse-scored Child Behavior Checklist [CBC; Achenbach & Rescorla, 2000] Aggression at age 3, *alpha* = .64; and CBC Aggression at prekindergarten, *alpha* = .65).

Table A.33. Overall predictive validity of total Parenting Interactions with Children: Checklist of Observations Linked to Outcomes (PICCOLO™) scores

	Cognitive-language outcomes		Cognitive-language-social outcomes	
	3 years	Prekindergarten	3 years	Prekindergarten
PICCOLO 1 year	.25**	.25**	.20**	.23**
PICCOLO 2 years	.27**	.27**	.24**	.24**
PICCOLO 3 years	.21**	.24**	.19**	.25**
PICCOLO 1–3 years	.27**	.28**	.21**	.26**

**p < .01; partial correlations, controlling for testing language (Spanish or English).

Statistically significant correlations between these constructed outcome variables and PICCOLO at each age, as well as PICCOLO averaged for the three ages, demonstrated that the PICCOLO measure predicts children's developmental outcomes (see Table A.33).

The psychometric properties of the PICCOLO measure have been tested and show considerable evidence of multiple aspects of reliability and validity. The items that make up PICCOLO can be reliably observed by non-experts with only a few hours of training. The four domains of PICCOLO—Affection, Responsiveness, Encouragement, and Teaching, represent reliable scales. The items show content validity, and the domains and total PICCOLO scores show construct validity. Finally, the domains and the total PICCOLO scores predict positive outcomes for children, particularly the cognitive, language, and social skills that underlie school readiness.

B

Spanish PICCOLO™ Tool

The Spanish PICCOLO™ Tool is provided on the following pages. Practitioners who speak Spanish as their first language may find it useful. Its primary advantage, however, is for practitioners to use with Spanish-speaking parents to discuss observations of their parenting behaviors in terms of their parenting strengths.

Interacción entre padres e hijos

Lista de control de observaciones enlazadas con resultados

INSTRUCCIONES: Observe detenidamente el comportamiento de los padres que estén tranquilos. La frecuencia es más importante que la complejidad, aunque la conducta compleja a menudo consta de varios ejemplos.

PUNTAJE: 0 "Ausente"—no se observa la conducta
1 "Raramente"—conducta breve, leve, o apenas emergiendo
2 "Claramente"—conducta definida, marcada, o frecuente

AFECTO
Cariño, acercamiento físico, y expresiones positivas hacia el niño/a

#	El padre o la madre...	Pautas para la observación	Ausente	Raramente	Claramente
1	habla con un tono de voz cariñoso	La voz del padre o la madre tiene un tono positivo y demuestra entusiasmo y ternura. Si el padre o la madre habla poco pero con cariño, debe dársele una puntuación alta.	0	1	2
2	sonríe al niño/a	El padre o la madre sonríe al niño/a pero no necesariamente se ven a los ojos cuando sonríe. Incluye las sonrisas leves.	0	1	2
3	elogia al niño/a	El padre o la madre dice algo positivo en cuanto al niño/a o a lo que éste hace. La palabra "gracias" se considera un elogio.	0	1	2
4	está físicamente cerca del niño/a	El padre o la madre está al alcance de la mano del niño/a, de manera que puede tranquilizarle o ayudarle cómodamente. Considere el contexto: se espera mayor cercanía para leer un libro que para jugar a la casita.	0	1	2
5	utiliza expresiones positivas con el niño/a	El padre o la madre dice cosas positivas o utiliza palabras como "mi amor", "bien hecho" o un sobrenombre afectuoso. (*Nota:* El énfasis está en las expresiones verbales).	0	1	2
6	se dedica de lleno a interactuar con el niño/a	El padre o la madre participa activamente *con* el niño/a, no solamente a las actividades o a otros adultos.	0	1	2
7	ofrece afecto emocional	El padre o la madre muestra placer, cariño u otro tipo de emoción positiva al niño/a y de forma directa hacia el niño/a. (*Nota:* Incluye expresiones verbales, pero haga hincapié en las expresiones no verbales).	0	1	2

COMENTARIOS:

Total de Afecto:

ID # _____ Nombre: _____ Fecha de nacimiento del niño/a: ____/____/____ Fecha de hoy: ____/____/____

 **PICCOLO**™

Interacción entre padres e hijos
Lista de control de observaciones enlazadas con resultados

INSTRUCCIONES: Observe detenidamente el comportamiento de los padres que estén tranquilos. La frecuencia es más importante que la complejidad, aunque la conducta compleja a menudo consta de varios ejemplos.

PUNTAJE: 0 "Ausente"—no se observa la conducta
1 "Raramente"—conducta breve, leve, o apenas emergiendo
2 "Claramente"—conducta definida, marcada, o frecuente

 ### RECEPTIVIDAD
Reacción ante señales, emociones, palabras, intereses, y conductas del niño/a

#	El padre o la madre...	Pautas para la observación	Ausente	Raramente	Claramente
1	presta atención a lo que hace el niño/a	El padre o la madre observa y reacciona ante lo que el niño/a hace, para lo cual hace comentarios, demuestra interés, brinda ayuda o atiende las acciones del niño/a de algún otro modo.	0	1	2
2	cambia el ritmo o la actividad para satisfacer los intereses o las necesidades del niño/a	El padre o la madre intenta una actividad nueva o acelera o disminuye el ritmo de la actividad en respuesta a la mirada del niño/a, a lo que éste toca, a lo que dice o a las emociones que demuestra.	0	1	2
3	es flexible ante el cambio de actividades o intereses del niño/a	El padre o la madre accede al deseo del niño/a de cambiar de actividad o de juguete, o demuestra estar de acuerdo con el cambio o con el hecho de que el niño/a juegue de forma poco usual con o sin juguetes.	0	1	2
4	sigue de cerca lo que el niño/a intenta hacer	El padre o la madre responde a las actividades del niño/a y participa en ellas.	0	1	2
5	reacciona ante las emociones del niño/a	El padre o la madre reacciona ante los sentimientos positivos o negativos del niño/a, para lo cual demuestra comprensión o aceptación, sugiere soluciones, hace que el niño/a retome la actividad, identifica o describe los sentimientos de éste, demuestra un sentimiento similar o brinda compasión ante los sentimientos negativos.	0	1	2
6	observa al niño/a cuando habla o hace ruidos	Cuando el niño/a hace ruidos, el padre o la madre dirige la mirada al rostro del niño/a o (si los ojos o el rostro del niño/a no están visibles) el padre o la madre cambia de posición y mueve el rostro hacia el niño/a.	0	1	2
7	responde a las palabras o los sonidos del niño/a	El padre o la madre repite lo que el niño/a dice o a los sonidos que hace, habla en cuanto a lo que el niño/a dice o podría estar diciendo o contesta las preguntas que le hace.	0	1	2

COMENTARIOS:

Total de Receptividad:

Spanish PICCOLO™ Tool by Lori A. Roggman, Gina A. Cook, Mark S. Innocenti, and Vonda Jump Norman, with Katie Christiansen. © 2013 by Paul H. Brookes Publishing Co., Inc. Todos los derechos reservados./All rights reserved. In *Parenting Interactions with Children: Checklist of Observations Linked to Outcomes (PICCOLO™) User's Guide* by Lori A. Roggman, Gina A. Cook, Mark S. Innocenti, Vonda Jump Norman, Katie Christiansen and Sheila Anderson. (2013; Paul H. Brookes Publishing Co., Inc.)

P I C C O L O ™

Interacción entre padres e hijos

Lista de control de observaciones enlazadas con resultados

INSTRUCCIONES: Observe detenidamente el comportamiento de los padres que estén tranquilos. La frecuencia es más importante que la complejidad, aunque la conducta compleja a menudo consta de varios ejemplos.

PUNTAJE: 0 "Ausente"—no se observa la conducta
1 "Raramente"—conducta breve, leve, o apenas emergiendo
2 "Claramente"—conducta definida, marcada, o frecuente

ALIENTO

Apoyo activo a la exploración, el esfuerzo, las destrezas, la iniciativa, la curiosidad, la creatividad, y el juego

#	El padre o la madre...	Pautas para la observación	Ausente	Raramente	Claramente
1	espera la reacción del niño/a tras hacer una sugerencia	El padre o la madre hace una pausa después de decir al niño/a lo que podría hacer y espera a que éste responda o haga algo, ya sea que el niño/a reaccione o no.	0	1	2
2	alienta al niño/a a tocar los juguetes	El padre o la madre ofrece los juguetes o dice cosas positivas cuando el niño/a demuestra obvio interés en ellos. (No incluye el prevenir que el niño/a se ponga los juguetes en la boca).	0	1	2
3	apoya al niño/a para que tome la iniciativa	El padre o la madre permite que el niño/a elija la actividad o el juguete y se involucra en la actividad o en el juguete que el niño/a elige en un momento determinado.	0	1	2
4	alienta al niño/a cuando hace cosas por su propia cuenta	El padre o la madre demuestra entusiasmo por las cosas que el niño/a intenta hacer sin ayuda, permite que éste elija la forma de hacer las cosas y le permite que intente hacerlas antes de ofrecerle ayuda o sugerencias. El padre o la madre podría involucrarse en las actividades que el niño/a "hace por su cuenta".	0	1	2
5	brinda aliento verbal a los esfuerzos del niño/a	El padre o la madre demuestra entusiasmo verbal, sus comentarios son positivos o hace sugerencias sobre las actividades del niño/a.	0	1	2
6	ofrece sugerencias para ayudar al niño/a	El padre o la madre da sugerencias o hace comentarios que *facilitan* las actividades sin interferir en el juego del niño/a.	0	1	2
7	demuestra entusiasmo hacia lo que el niño/a hace	El padre o la madre hace comentarios positivos, aplaude o tiene otras reacciones positivas ante lo que el niño/a *hace*, incluso con entusiasmo silencioso, como por ejemplo, da palmaditas, asiente con la cabeza, sonríe o hace preguntas al niño/a sobre las actividades.	0	1	2

COMENTARIOS:

Total de Aliento:

ID # _____ Nombre:_____ Fecha de nacimiento del niño/a: _____/_____/_____ Fecha de hoy: _____/_____/_____

Interacción entre padres e hijos

Lista de control de observaciones enlazadas con resultados

INSTRUCCIONES: Observe detenidamente el comportamiento de los padres que estén tranquilos. La frecuencia es más importante que la complejidad, aunque la conducta compleja a menudo consta de varios ejemplos.

PUNTAJE: 0 "Ausente"—no se observa la conducta
1 "Raramente"—conducta breve, leve, o apenas emergiendo
2 "Claramente"—conducta definida, marcada, o frecuente

ENSEÑANZA
Conversación y juego compartidos, estímulo cognitivo, explicaciones, y preguntas

#	El padre o la madre...	Pautas para la observación	Ausente	Raramente	Claramente
1	explica las razones de las cosas al niño/a	El padre o la madre da una explicación que podría ser la respuesta a una pregunta de "por qué", ya sea que el niño/a pregunte o no.	0	1	2
2	sugiere actividades que amplían lo que el niño/a hace	El padre o la madre sugiere al niño/a lo que podría hacer para ampliar lo que ya está haciendo, pero no interrumpe el interés, las acciones o el juego del niño/a.	0	1	2
3	repite o amplía las palabras o los sonidos del niño/a	El padre o la madre repite las mismas palabras o hace los mismos sonidos que hace el niño/a o repite lo que éste dice a la vez que agrega palabras o amplía la idea.	0	1	2
4	nombra los objetos o las acciones al niño/a	El padre o la madre dice el nombre de lo que el niño/a hace, de lo que toca o de lo que ve.	0	1	2
5	participa en los juegos imaginarios del niño/a	El padre o la madre participa en los juegos imaginarios de cualquier forma; por ejemplo, "come" la comida imaginaria.	0	1	2
6	realiza las actividades en una secuencia de pasos	El padre o la madre demuestra o describe el orden de los pasos o realiza la actividad de manera que los pasos sean obvios aunque no explique los pasos con exactitud. Se cuenta la lectura de libros *solamente* si el padre o la madre es explícito con los pasos mediante la exageración o la explicación de los pasos al leer.	0	1	2
7	explica al niño/a las características de los objetos	El padre o la madre utiliza palabras o frases que describen detalles como el color, la forma, la textura, el movimiento, la función u otras características.	0	1	2
8	pide información al niño/a	El padre o la madre hace preguntas o dice "dime", "muéstrame" o cualquier otra indicación que precise una respuesta de si o no, una respuesta breve o una respuesta larga, independientemente de si el niño/a responde o no. No incluye las preguntas para centrar la atención ("¿ves?") o para sugerir actividades ("¿quieres abrir la bolsa?").	0	1	2

COMENTARIOS:

Total de Enseñanza:

Spanish PICCOLO™ Tool by Lori A. Roggman, Gina A. Cook, Mark S. Innocenti, and Vonda Jump Norman, with Katie Christiansen. © 2013 by Paul H. Brookes Publishing Co., Inc.
Todos los derechos reservados./All rights reserved. In *Parenting Interactions with Children: Checklist of Observations Linked to Outcomes (PICCOLO™) User's Guide*
by Lori A. Roggman, Gina A. Cook, Mark S. Innocenti, Vonda Jump Norman, Katie Christiansen and Sheila Anderson. (2013; Paul H. Brookes Publishing Co., Inc.)

C

The PICCOLO™ Training DVD Video Clip Scores

PICCOLO scores and the rationale for each item's score are provided for the video clips on *The PICCOLO™ Training DVD: Implementation and Scoring* (Roggman et al., 2013).

ONE-MINUTE OBSERVATION: AFFECTION

Item	Code	Rationale
Affection 1	2	The mother uses a warm voice throughout.
Affection 2	2	The mother smiles often. One smile is directed at the child.
Affection 3	2	The mother says, "You're right," and "Yeah, he did!"
Affection 4	2	The child is sitting on the mother's lap throughout.
Affection 5	0	The mother uses no positive expressions.
Affection 6	2	The mother is engaged with what the child is looking at and talking about in the book.
Affection 7	2	The mother seems to really enjoy her time with her child.
Responsiveness 1	2	The mother pays attention to what the child is looking at in the book and responds.
Responsiveness 2	2	The mother asks questions about food to maintain the child's interest and changes the pace of the book by reading some of it and paraphrasing other parts.
Responsiveness 3	2	The child says, "Look," and directs the mother's attention to another page and away from the food. The mother allows the child to flip the pages when she is done.
Responsiveness 4	2	The mother responds to what the child talks about in the book and gets involved by explaining and elaborating.
Responsiveness 5	2	The mother gets excited when the child gets excited about the book. The child gets a little concerned about cheese being healthy, and the mother reassures her.
Responsiveness 6	0	The mother looks at the child in the very beginning and end but NOT when the child makes a noise.
Responsiveness 7	2	The mother replies to almost everything the child says.
Encouragement 1	2	The mother asks many questions ("Is there anything healthy you like to eat?") and waits patiently for an answer.
Encouragement 2	1	The mother says positive things when the child shows interest in the book.
Encouragement 3	1	The mother does not offer choices, but she does get involved with the child's interest in the book.

Item	Code	Rationale
Encouragement 4	2	The mother lets the child choose which items in the book to talk about and shows enthusiasm when the child correctly identifies the watermelon.
Encouragement 5	2	The mother says, "You're right. He did!" when the child is trying to find something healthy.
Encouragement 6	0	The mother offers no suggestions.
Encouragement 7	2	The mother nods, smiles, and asks many questions.
Teaching 1	0	The mother does not explain reasons to the child.
Teaching 2	1	The mother says, "Is there anything you like to eat?"
Teaching 3	2	The mother says, "Cheese is healthy," "muffins," "pie," and "leaf."
Teaching 4	2	The mother labels *sausage, salami, sandwiches,* and *caterpillar.*
Teaching 5	0	The mother does not engage in pretend play.
Teaching 6	0	The mother does not do activities in a sequence of steps.
Teaching 7	1	The mother says, "big," "fat," "caterpillar," and "healthy."
Teaching 8	2	The mother asks, "Is there anything healthy you like to eat?" "What's that?" "What did he eat through?" and "What is he now?"

ONE-MINUTE OBSERVATION: RESPONSIVENESS

Item	Code	Rationale
Affection 1	2	The mother uses a very warm, inviting voice.
Affection 2	2	The mother smiles several times, almost constantly throughout.
Affection 3	2	The mother says, "Ummm," "Good job," and "I think it tastes yummy."
Affection 4	2	The mother is definitely within arm's reach for the majority of the time and gets the child to come next to her.
Affection 5	0	The mother uses no positive expressions.
Affection 6	2	The mother is actively involved with the child.
Affection 7	2	The mother seems to really enjoy the play.
Responsiveness 1	2	The mother is constantly aware of the child and makes lots of statements.
Responsiveness 2	2	The mother changes pace by suggesting other things to add on to the play, such as stirring the food and tasting it.
Responsiveness 3	2	The mother is flexible about the child wanting the mother to sip first before her and lets the child stir.
Responsiveness 4	2	The mother follows and gets involved with the child's activities.
Responsiveness 5	2	The mother responds to the child's wanting to stir and matches emotions (laughs).
Responsiveness 6	2	The mother looks most of the time.
Responsiveness 7	2	The mother replies to almost everything the child says.
Encouragement 1	2	The mother says, "Can I have a sip?" then waits for child to bring the cup over. She says, "Bring it closer. I wanna taste."
Encouragement 2	2	The mother allows the child to play and encourages her to do things on her own with toys. She says, "You wanna sip?" (offers cup to child).
Encouragement 3	2	The mother asks the child what she wants to do and goes along with everything the child chooses.
Encouragement 4	2	The mother shows enthusiasm, lets the child choose how things are done, and allows her to try before helping.
Encouragement 5	2	The mother says, "Good job" and "Tastes yummy."
Encouragement 6	0	The mother offers no suggestions to help the child.

Item	Code	Rationale
Encouragement 7	2	The mother makes positive responses, smiles, and seems overall enthusiastic.
Teaching 1	1	The mother says, "Bring it closer. I wanna taste."
Teaching 2	2	The mother says, "Did you need to heat it up some more?" and "Stir it up some more?"
Teaching 3	2	The mother repeats "a sip" and "You do it."
Teaching 4	2	The mother labels *sip, food, stir,* and *taste.* (She labels all of the actions done in the 1 minute.)
Teaching 5	2	The mother eats food, stirs, and heats up the food.
Teaching 6	1	The mother stirs and then tastes the food.
Teaching 7	1	The mother says, "Tastes yummy," but it is about the pretend play, so it is not a real characteristic.
Teaching 8	1	The mother asks, "Can I have a sip?" ("Do you need to heat it up?" was more of a suggestion.)

ONE-MINUTE OBSERVATION: ENCOURAGEMENT

Item	Code	Rationale
Affection 1	2	The mother uses a warm and affectionate voice.
Affection 2	2	The mother smiles throughout.
Affection 3	2	The mother says, "You can do it!" and "yay!"
Affection 4	2	The child is in the mother's lap.
Affection 5	1	The mother says, "baby."
Affection 6	2	The mother is warmly and actively engaged in a game with the baby and his socks.
Affection 7	2	The mother laughs and smiles and seems to really enjoy the play.
Responsiveness 1	2	The mother is aware and makes lots of comments about the child trying to take off his socks.
Responsiveness 2	2	The mother switches socks at a good pace, slows things down and speeds things up, and tries to get the child to put the sock on instead of always pulling it off.
Responsiveness 3	1	The mother allows the child to keep the sock and hold it while she is trying to put it on his foot.
Responsiveness 4	2	The mother sees what the child wants, responds, and does what the child wants. She says, "Other foot?"
Responsiveness 5	2	The mother matches the child's emotions.
Responsiveness 6	1	The mother seems to look at the baby when the baby makes noise, but she mostly looks at the activity.
Responsiveness 7	2	The mother repeats the "uhh" sounds. She replies to the screaming.
Encouragement 1	2	The mother waits when she wants the child to take his sock off.
Encouragement 2	2	The mother offers socks to the child.
Encouragement 3	2	The mother goes along with what the child does with the sock and says, "Other foot?"
Encouragement 4	2	The mother lets the child choose which foot. She is not intrusive, and she shows enthusiasm when the child pulls the sock off. She waits to give help.
Encouragement 5	2	The mother says, "Come on," "You can do it," "almost," and "yay!"
Encouragement 6	1	The mother tells the child, "Put your foot up" (to help get sock on).
Encouragement 7	2	The mother shows lots of enthusiasm about the child's efforts to take off his socks. The mother says, "Come on; you can do it" and "almost."

Item	Code	Rationale
Teaching 1	0	The mother does not explain reasons to the child.
Teaching 2	2	The mother suggests pulling off the sock or putting it on.
Teaching 3	2	The mother repeats the child's grunts and giggles.
Teaching 4	2	The mother labels *sock*, *foot*, and the actions *put it on* and *take it off*.
Teaching 5	0	The mother does not engage in pretend play.
Teaching 6	1	The mother puts on the sock and then pulls it off.
Teaching 7	1	The mother talks about on, off, and other foot.
Teaching 8	0	The mother uses no information-seeking questions.

ONE-MINUTE OBSERVATION: TEACHING

Item	Code	Rationale
Affection 1	2	The mother's voice is warm.
Affection 2	0	The mother's smiles are not directed at the child.
Affection 3	2	The mother says, "Thank you," "There ya go," and "You're a good cook."
Affection 4	2	The mother moves to be closer to the child when needed.
Affection 5	0	The mother does not use positive expressions.
Affection 6	2	The mother is involved with the child's activities.
Affection 7	2	The mother seems to enjoy playtime and seems fond of the child.
Responsiveness 1	2	The mother could narrate what the child is doing. She is very aware of the child's activity.
Responsiveness 2	2	The mother goes to the cooking toys when the child looks at them and adds a little to the play.
Responsiveness 3	2	The mother is flexible when the child wants to go back to the cooking toys, and the mother gets involved.
Responsiveness 4	2	The mother lets the child lead the play.
Responsiveness 5	2	The mother shows similar emotions as the child. She shows understanding about what the child wants.
Responsiveness 6	2	The mother is already looking when the child speaks much of the time. She turns to look at her about half of the time.
Responsiveness 7	2	The mother replies each time the child says something. She says, "baby's food" and "Oh, you're gonna put it in my bowl."
Encouragement 1	2	The mother clearly waits after asking the child something. She says, "Do you wanna get your baby and feed her?" She is very patient throughout.
Encouragement 2	2	The mother offers some toys, makes positive statements, and is very encouraging with the cooking toys.
Encouragement 3	2	The mother allows the child to choose what they do and gets involved with what the child chooses.
Encouragement 4	1	The child does not try to do anything on her own, but her mother allows her to choose what is done and lets the child try things first.
Encouragement 5	2	The mother says, "There ya go," and "good cook."
Encouragement 6	0	The mother does not suggest anything to make it easier for the child.
Encouragement 7	2	The mother has quiet enthusiasm. She asks a lot of questions and makes lots of positive comments and statements.
Teaching 1	0	The mother provides no reasons.
Teaching 2	2	The mother says, "Do you wanna get your baby and feed her?"
Teaching 3	2	The mother says, "baby's food," and "Oh, you're gonna put it in my bowl."

Item	Code	Rationale
Teaching 4	2	The mother says, "Noah," "Noah's wife," "bowl," "peas," and "food."
Teaching 5	2	The mother makes eating noises multiple times and talks about the food afterward.
Teaching 6	0	The mother does not do activities in a sequence.
Teaching 7	1	The mother talks about the baby's food.
Teaching 8	2	The mother asks, "What are those?" and "Do you wanna feed her some of that food?"

FIVE-MINUTE OBSERVATION: PRACTICE 1

Item	Code	Rationale
Affection 1	2	The mother has a warm voice that shows affection.
Affection 2	2	The mother smiles several times throughout.
Affection 3	2	Not all of the times the mother says "thanks" and "yay" are praising, but there are enough for a score of 2.
Affection 4	2	The mother is always close enough to the child. Even when she sits on the floor, she stays really close.
Affection 5	0	The mother uses no positive expressions.
Affection 6	2	The mother stays involved and engaged with the child even though she is pretty directive of the play. It does not seem to intrude on what the child wants.
Affection 7	2	The mother shows enjoyment and fondness, especially when the child does something correctly and gets a "yay!"
Responsiveness 1	2	The mother is aware and constantly makes comments.
Responsiveness 2	1	The mother changes pace a few times, but it is not clear if it is in response to the child's interests.
Responsiveness 3	1	The child does not have many choices about the activity, but the mother is flexible with the plates and then counting the blocks on the plate.
Responsiveness 4	2	The mother follows what the child is trying to do and gets involved. For example, when the child starts putting blocks on the plate, the mother counts them with him.
Responsiveness 5	1	The mother shows similar emotions throughout, and she does try to reengage the child but does not necessarily reengage positively.
Responsiveness 6	2	The mother is constantly looking at the child but makes extra effort when the child speaks.
Responsiveness 7	2	There is a really great dialogue between the mother and child. The mother replies to almost all of what the child says.
Encouragement 1	1	The mother is patient when asking about colors but does not wait for most other suggestions.
Encouragement 2	2	The mother really encourages the child to play with toys, especially the ring toys and the cups and blocks.
Encouragement 3	1	The mother is very directive of the play, and the child has few choices. The child chooses to repeat putting the blocks on the plate and counting them, and the mother gets involved and helps count.
Encouragement 4	1	The mother shows enthusiasm for things the child does without help—the ring toys.
Encouragement 5	2	The mother offers lots of verbal enthusiasm. She says, "yay" a lot.
Encouragement 6	0	The mother offers no suggestions.
Encouragement 7	2	The mother shows lots of clear enthusiasm, especially with hand clapping, saying "yay," and smiling.

Item	Code	Rationale
Teaching 1	1	The mother says, "You probably think it's candy cuz of all the colors," and "No more juice; you already drunk it all." These are not very long explanations: simple and short.
Teaching 2	1	Lots of the mother's suggestions barely extend beyond what the child is already doing. She did suggest to continue counting and labeling colors.
Teaching 3	2	The mother says, "Want your dada?" "It fell," "four," and "two." She also says, "yeah," a couple of times.
Teaching 4	2	The mother offers lots of labels throughout. She labels almost everything.
Teaching 5	0	The mother does not engage in pretend play.
Teaching 6	0	The mother does no activities in a sequence.
Teaching 7	2	Some colors are labels, but the mother still uses lots of other colors and makes a strong effort to count lots of items. The mother says, "Food goes on plate," and "One for you; one for me."
Teaching 8	2	The mother asks the child to count. She says, "Is this green?" "I can't have one?" "You put your food on a plate, right?" "And then this is your cup right?" "So you gonna give me some on my plate?" and "What else you use this for?"

FIVE-MINUTE OBSERVATION: PRACTICE 2

Item	Code	Rationale
Affection 1	2	The mother has a warm voice.
Affection 2	2	There are a lot of smiles throughout the clip. Big smiles are shared.
Affection 3	2	The mother says, "good job," "yay," "good," and "That's right."
Affection 4	2	The mother is close to the child.
Affection 5	0	The mother used no positive expressions.
Affection 6	2	The mother asks questions, follows the child's lead, and plays with the child the entire time.
Affection 7	2	The mother is fond of the child, enjoys this time, and smiles.
Responsiveness 1	2	The mother makes many comments, reacts to the child, and is aware of what the child is doing and saying.
Responsiveness 2	2	The mother slows down the block building and adds to the play to keep it going. The mother begins the pretend play when the child does not know what to do next.
Responsiveness 3	2	The mother lets the child direct the play (plays along) and asks permission before adding to the play.
Responsiveness 4	2	The mother makes comments, responds to the child, and helps her build.
Responsiveness 5	2	The mother matches emotions and understands when the child says no (multiple times).
Responsiveness 6	1	The mother hardly looks the first half, but the second half she looks pretty consistently.
Responsiveness 7	2	There is a great dialogue between the child and mother. The mother consistently replies.
Encouragement 1	2	The mother waits after giving suggestions and waits for the child to do or say something before acting.
Encouragement 2	2	The mother offers blocks and praises once a task is done.
Encouragement 3	2	The mother offers choices and gets and stays involved with the play.
Encouragement 4	2	The mother lets the child choose how things are done. She lets the child struggle before helping and shows enthusiasm.

Item	Code	Rationale
Encouragement 5	2	The mother says, "That's a pretty cool looking house," "That's good," "There it goes," "good," and "oh, nice."
Encouragement 6	1	The mother says, "Push it in hard," but makes no other suggestions.
Encouragement 7	2	The mother asks many questions, smiles, and makes positive comments.
Teaching 1	1	The mother says, "Put roof on top cuz we don't want the rain to get them wet."
Teaching 2	1	The mother asks, "Now should we make a roof for the house?"
Teaching 3	2	The mother says, "right there," "and the trains," "bigger," "There's only one spot," "Now I can do one?" "not sleepy," "museum," and "not gonna work."
Teaching 4	2	The mother labels everything that the child and mother are playing with. Even though they play with only a few items, she labels everything and labels the activities during pretend play.
Teaching 5	2	The mother engages in extensive pretend play with the house.
Teaching 6	2	The mother says, "Play kids go in bedroom," "Go to sleep," "Snore," "Sun comes up," "Rooster crows," "They wake up," and "Eat chicken for breakfast."
Teaching 7	1	The mother says that the museum blocks were huge. She says, "under the roof," "bigger," and "smaller."
Teaching 8	2	The mother asks, "Were they bigger or smaller?" "Who's gonna cook it?" "Is this where he's gonna sleep?" "Does that look good?" and many other questions.

FIVE-MINUTE OBSERVATION: PRACTICE 3

Item	Code	Rationale
Affection 1	2	The mother's voice is warm.
Affection 2	2	The mother smiles frequently.
Affection 3	2	The mother says, "good job," "There you go," "yeah," "You got it," and "You've mastered the toy."
Affection 4	2	The mother and child are very close throughout.
Affection 5	2	The mother says, "sweetie" and "kiddo" (many times for both).
Affection 6	2	The mother makes comments and helps the child when needed.
Affection 7	2	The mother consoles the child when upset and seems fond of the child.
Responsiveness 1	2	The mother makes many comments. She reacts to the child's actions and words.
Responsiveness 2	1	The mother slows down the pace with the blocks so the child can get them in but she could have changed the activity in response to the child's frustration.
Responsiveness 3	2	The mother lets the child choose how to place blocks in and which blocks to play with. She stays involved.
Responsiveness 4	2	The mother hands the child toys. She is constantly responding and follows what the child is trying to do with the shapes.
Responsiveness 5	2	The mother says, "Want some juice?" and "What's wrong?" She comforts the child when the child is fussy.
Responsiveness 6	1	The mother looks at the child occasionally.
Responsiveness 7	2	The mother responds to the child's sounds and words and talks about what the child could be saying.
Encouragement 1	1	The mother says, "Try one of the squares," and "Wanna do it again?" but the mother is a little grabby at times.

Item	Code	Rationale
Encouragement 2	2	The mother hands toys to the child and encourages the child to keep trying.
Encouragement 3	2	The mother lets the child choose which blocks to play with and stays involved with the child.
Encouragement 4	2	The mother is enthusiastic about the child getting shapes in the can on her own. She offers suggestions after the child struggles a little.
Encouragement 5	2	The mother says, "You did it," "almost," and "There you go" many times.
Encouragement 6	2	The mother offers suggestions many times. She says, "Turn it this way," and "Keep turning."
Encouragement 7	2	The mother smiles, pats the child, asks a few questions, and makes positive comments about the child's actions.
Teaching 1	0	The mother does not explain reasons.
Teaching 2	2	The mother says, "Empty it out," "Try one of the squares," "triangles," and "Put them in their holes."
Teaching 3	1	The mother repeats "empty."
Teaching 4	2	The mother labels *triangle, square, circle, ABCs,* and *lid.* She labels everything the child plays with.
Teaching 5	0	The mother does not engage in pretend play.
Teaching 6	0	The mother does not do activities in a sequence of steps.
Teaching 7	1	The mother says, "triangle," "hole," and "empty."
Teaching 8	1	The mother asks, "Which is the triangle hole?" and "Do you need juice?"

FIVE-MINUTE OBSERVATION: PRACTICE 4

Item	Code	Rationale
Affection 1	2	The mother has a warm voice.
Affection 2	2	The mother smiles frequently.
Affection 3	2	The mother says, "yeah," "That's right," "very good," "You took it off," and "You know what to do, don't you?"
Affection 4	2	The mother and child are close throughout.
Affection 5	1	The mother says, "You silly."
Affection 6	2	The mother is involved with the child through the whole clip.
Affection 7	2	The mother laughs, smiles, and seems to enjoy the time.
Responsiveness 1	2	The mother makes many comments. Her focus is on the child.
Responsiveness 2	2	The mother slows down the book when child wants to see the dog. She suggests new activities when there is a lull in play. The pace is good.
Responsiveness 3	2	The mother allows the child to throw toys. She plays along and lets the child choose how to do things.
Responsiveness 4	2	The mother responds to the child's actions and what the child tries to say. She participates in activities.
Responsiveness 5	2	The mother mirrors smiles and laughs. The mother's and child's emotions are matched.
Responsiveness 6	2	The mother looks at the child for most of the child's sounds.
Responsiveness 7	2	The mother says, "dog" (several times) and "uh oh" (several times) and replies to most of what the child says.
Encouragement 1	2	The mother waits after saying, "Can you take the lid off?" "Can you get that one?" and "Do this one."

Item	Code	Rationale
Encouragement 2	2	The mother offers many toys to the child. She matches the child's excitement when the child gets excited about the toys.
Encouragement 3	2	The mother lets the child choose how to put the animals in the boat and gets involved. She gets involved by repeating "dog" while looking at the book.
Encouragement 4	2	The mother shows enthusiasm and lets the child choose how to do things.
Encouragement 5	2	The mother says, "You did it," "Do it again," and "You know what to do with that."
Encouragement 6	0	The mother offers no suggestions.
Encouragement 7	2	The mother smiles, asks questions, and gives positive statements.
Teaching 1	0	The mother does not explain reasons.
Teaching 2	1	The mother suggests taking the lid off and pulling items out of the bag, but she could have suggested a lot more activities.
Teaching 3	2	The mother repeats "dog" (multiple times) and "uh oh" (multiple times). This is all the child says.
Teaching 4	1	The mother labels *dog, spoon, lid,* and *knob,* but they had a lot of toys out that she could have labeled and did not.
Teaching 5	0	The mother does not engage in pretend play.
Teaching 6	1	The mother repeats the sequence of walking up the ladder, falling in, and saying, "uh oh."
Teaching 7	0	The mother does not talk to the child about characteristics of objects.
Teaching 8	2	The mother asks, "Can you…?" "What is it?" "Do you see a dog?" "What is in there?" "What do you see?" and "Can you get it?"

TEN-MINUTE OBSERVATION: EXAMPLE A

Item	Code	Rationale
Affection 1	1	At times, the mother is warm and encouraging, but she is not really inviting.
Affection 2	1	The mother gives a small smile in the beginning and one big one, but she mostly does not smile.
Affection 3	2	The mother says, "yeah," "There you go," "all right" (twice), and "good job" (twice).
Affection 4	2	The mother is near the child most of the time.
Affection 5	0	The mother does not say any positive expressions.
Affection 6	2	The mother has reciprocal interactions with the child. She is aware of what the child is doing and helps with the child's play. She is involved with the child by talking even though she is doing her own activity.
Affection 7	1	The mother shows a little bit of warmth and enthusiasm.
Responsiveness 1	2	Although the mother is playing with toys, she would still be able to narrate what the child is doing, and she is involved with what the child wants to do with the toys.
Responsiveness 2	2	The activity changes are really subtle (we are unsure of how often they are in response to the child). There are pauses in which the mother changes pace or introduces new activities.
Responsiveness 3	2	The mother is very flexible about what the child wants to do. She says, "Oh, fine. Only one goes on there at a time?" She lets the child take the train in and out of the cube she made to put the train in.
Responsiveness 4	1	The mother responds to the child's activities and choices; however, she could get more involved with his activities.

Item	Code	Rationale
Responsiveness 5	1	The mother matches the child's emotions; however, she becomes less and less enthusiastic with the child toward the end of the video clip.
Responsiveness 6	1	The mother looks up occasionally or is already looking at the child; however, there are times when the child is speaking and wants her to look and she does not.
Responsiveness 7	2	The mother replies to many words and sounds. She consistently replies "huh" or "hmm" every time the child says, "Hey, Mama."
Encouragement 1	1	The mother does not wait the majority of the time and tends to intrude with the blocks more and more. She does wait occasionally with the book and somewhat with the blocks.
Encouragement 2	2	The mother offers toys and encourages the child's play when he holds up the choo choo train.
Encouragement 3	1	The mother does not get too involved with what the child chooses.
Encouragement 4	1	The mother shows enthusiasm for things the child tries without help. She says, "Good job" when he fixes the bridge all by himself. She lets the child choose how to do things: "Oh, fine. Only one goes on there at a time? Not two." She often jumps in before the child has a chance to really try accomplishing a task. She lets him try for a second, then she helps or does it for him.
Encouragement 5	2	The mother says, "all right" (two times), "good job" (two times), "There you go," and "You gonna help me make a house?" She sounds encouraging.
Encouragement 6	0	The mother does not make anything easier for the child.
Encouragement 7	2	The mother makes positive statements ("good job," "That is a choo choo train!"). She smiles and asks questions. The mother changes the pitch in her voice to make it more enthusiastic.
Teaching 1	1	The mother says, "Lift up the bridge so that mine can get out."
Teaching 2	1	The mother suggests building a road. Most suggestions are not about what the child is already doing and seem intrusive.
Teaching 3	2	The mother repeats "race," and "choo choo train." Because choo choo train is repeated so many times, this item is coded higher.
Teaching 4	2	The mother labels book pictures and colors as well as *choo choo train, road, bridge, house, block,* and *turnaround*. Although she does not have very many labels, she consistently labels what they are doing in the play and what they are playing with.
Teaching 5	1	The mother says, "beep beep" with the racing car and choo choo train—all very subtle.
Teaching 6	0	No activities are done in a sequence. Road building is not a sequence, simply a repetition of putting pieces together. Nothing distinct is done first, second, and so forth.
Teaching 7	2	The mother describes a good variety of characteristics: "purple" (instead of green), "1, 2, 3," "looks like a box," "The [caterpillar] got fat," and "Like a puzzle."
Teaching 8	2	The mother asks, "What is that?" "Is that a turnaround?" "How many of these are in this?" "Will you give me a block?" "Can you see my choo choo train in there?" "What is that? A square?" "What color is this?" and "What does a choo choo train say?"

TEN-MINUTE OBSERVATION: EXAMPLE B

Item	Code	Rationale
Affection 1	2	The mother speaks warmly toward the child.
Affection 2	2	The mothers smiles big and laughs.

Item	Code	Rationale
Affection 3	1	The mother says, "yeah" (some are not really praise) and "There you go."
Affection 4	2	The mother is near the child and tries to be near the child even though the child is all over the place.
Affection 5	2	The mother says, "girl," "little doctor girl," "girly," and "baby" (twice).
Affection 6	2	The mother maintains involvement with the child by trying to get the child involved with activities.
Affection 7	2	The mother shows fondness for the child and has positive emotions directed toward the child.
Responsiveness 1	2	The mother could narrate what the child is doing. She definitely pays more attention to the child rather than the toys.
Responsiveness 2	2	The mother tries to reengage the child and get her to sit on the floor. She changes activities when the child seems bored. She goes on to the next bag and slows the book down.
Responsiveness 3	2	The mother allows the child to play how she wants. The child hit the toy on the wall. The mother suggests activities such as checking mom's heart, but the child does not do it, and the mother accepts.
Responsiveness 4	1	The mother responds but is not physically involved with the child-initiated activities. She could have done more to be involved in what the child wanted to do. She does respond verbally and shifts to playing with the syringe (from the stethoscope) to follow the child's interest and notices the child using the object as a microphone.
Responsiveness 5	2	The mother mirrors the child's smiling and laughing. She reengages the child when she seems bored.
Responsiveness 6	2	The mother makes a real effort to look at the child when the child makes sounds.
Responsiveness 7	2	The mother replies to the sounds the child makes and the words she says ("a bubble," "knock-knock"). She talks a lot about what the child could be saying or doing.
Encouragement 1	1	During the book reading, she waits for a response; however, during the rest of the play, she does not look for a response or she already starts the activity.
Encouragement 2	2	The mother asks, "You wanna do it?" and offers the blood pressure toy. She gives lots of toys and allows the child to play in unusual ways. She shows and hands the child toys.
Encouragement 3	1	The mother does not really get involved with the activities the child chooses but shows some involvement by narrating the play and commenting on what the child chooses to do.
Encouragement 4	1	The mother shows enthusiasm but does not give the child a great opportunity to try things on her own. She does allow the child to choose how some things are done.
Encouragement 5	1	The mother says, "There you go," and "yeah."
Encouragement 6	1	The mother says, "Push it" (with the blocks), but she intrudes shortly after: "Do it hard."
Encouragement 7	2	The mother is very enthusiastic. She smiles, makes positive comments, and asks lots of questions.
Teaching 1	1	The mother says, "Come here so you can check mommy's heart-beat," but this is a weak explanation because it is more of a suggestion of something the child can do than a reason. Descriptions of the doctor toys are reflected in the score for Teaching Item 7.
Teaching 2	1	The mother suggests activities for the doctor toys ("Check heart-beat," "Wanna try blood pressure"). She also says, "Stack 'em up," and "Build a home."

Item	Code	Rationale
Teaching 3	1	The mother repeats "knock-knock, " and "bubble."
Teaching 4	2	The mother labels *caterpillar, sun, moon, apple, pear, plum, straw-berries,* and *blood pressure thing.* She labels throughout the video clip.
Teaching 5	1	The mother plays with the doctor toys and encourages the child working on the sick couch.
Teaching 6	2	The mother takes the blood pressure in sequence, saying "Let me show what the blood pressure cuff do. You put it on your arm, and then you go like this: *ch ch ch ch.* And this tighten up on you. Then, it check your blood pressure. Isn't that neat? You wanna do it? Here, you do it."
Teaching 7	2	The mother explains the function of the blood pressure toy. She talks about the green leaf, two pears, five oranges, and the colors of blocks (yellow and blue). She asks, "Did you eat those this week?" and says, "Couch must be sick."
Teaching 8	2	The mother asks, "Is that a green leaf?" "Is this his home?" "Where you going?" "Where do you see a bubble?" "What color is that?" "Do you see yourself in there?" "Did you check the heart?" and "They stack; did you know that?"

TEN-MINUTE OBSERVATION: CHILD WITH DISABILITY

Item	Code	Rationale
Affection 1	2	The mother uses a warm tone of voice.
Affection 2	2	The mother smiles constantly.
Affection 3	2	The mother says, "good reaching," "good job," "yay!" and several other positive comments.
Affection 4	2	The child is sitting in the mother's lap.
Affection 5	2	The mother says, "silly," "You silly," "little monkey," and "monkey."
Affection 6	2	The mother engages and interacts with the child as much as she can.
Affection 7	2	The mother seems to really enjoy the play with her body language, smiles, and kisses.
Responsiveness 1	2	The mother watches the child and reacts to what he is holding and doing.
Responsiveness 2	2	The mother tries picking up the pace with Peekaboo, hitting the coins together, pushing the coin in, and so forth.
Responsiveness 3	2	When the mother asks her child to do something and the child does something else, the mother is agreeable. She also lets the child play in unusual ways by grabbing the toy with his feet.
Responsiveness 4	2	The mother responds to what the child is doing and tries to get involved the best she can.
Responsiveness 5	2	The mother labels feelings, shows understanding, and tries to reengage the child.
Responsiveness 6	2	The mother is usually already looking at the child when he makes sounds.
Responsiveness 7	2	The mother replies to what the child could be saying and replies to his fussiness.
Encouragement 1	2	The mother always gives the child the opportunity to do what she suggested.
Encouragement 2	2	The mother constantly hands the child toys and lets him decide how to play with them.
Encouragement 3	2	The mother gives the child a choice and then gets involved by talking about what he did.

Item	Code	Rationale
Encouragement 4	2	The mother lets the child choose and lets the child struggle before offering help.
Encouragement 5	2	The mother says, "You can do it," "That's no problem," "You can get it now," and other verbal encouragement.
Encouragement 6	1	The mother says, "Push it."
Encouragement 7	2	The mother smiles, makes positive comments, and pats child.
Teaching 1	0	The mother offers no reasons.
Teaching 2	2	The mother says, "Push the coins in," "open," "close," and "clap together."
Teaching 3	0	The mother does not repeat any sounds. We decided that laughing is not counted as repeating.
Teaching 4	2	The mother labels everything they play with: *coins, monkey, pig, color,* and *nose.*
Teaching 5	0	The mother does not engage in pretend play.
Teaching 6	1	The mother puts a coin in and says a number (repeated).
Teaching 7	2	The mother says, "green one," "closed," "open," "1, 2, 3," and "baby cow."
Teaching 8	2	The mother asks, "Are you gonna get up?" "Are you done with the pig?" "Can you reach it?" "What's the matter?" and "What is that?" She asks a lot of "can you" questions. She also asks, "Do you want help?" and "Is that her nose?"

ONE-MINUTE OBSERVATION: SPANISH

Item	Code	Rationale
Affection 1	2	The mother speaks often in a kind, warm tone.
Affection 2	2	The mother smiles, laughs, and looks up at the child both early on and later in the video clip.
Affection 3	0	The mother never offers any direct praise for something that the child does.
Affection 4	2	The mother is sitting within arm's reach of the child. She leans in toward the child on multiple occasions.
Affection 5	0	The parent never uses an affectionate nickname or positive expression directed at the child or her actions.
Affection 6	2	The mother talks about the activities with the child, pays attention to everything the child does, and makes suggestions.
Affection 7	2	The mother smiles and laughs.
Responsiveness 1	2	The mother watches the child and responds throughout.
Responsiveness 2	2	The child stalls about halfway through, and the mother suggests a new activity. The mother makes suggestions later but does not force them when the child says no.
Responsiveness 3	2	As noted for the previous item, the mother makes suggestions but never forces the child to do one thing or another.
Responsiveness 4	2	The mother turns the house so that the child can continue playing with the animal.
Responsiveness 5	2	The mother laughs when the child laughs and smiles when the child smiles.
Responsiveness 6	2	The mother looks at the child consistently throughout the video clip.
Responsiveness 7	2	The mother replies to the child's words several times. She says, "¿Todos se durmieron? ¿Y a qué vamos a hacer?" [They're all sleeping? And what are we going to do?]; "¿No? OK" [Okay]; and "¿Esta muy rico?" [They're very delicious?].

Item	Code	Rationale
Encouragement 1	2	When the mother suggests that the child read the toys a book, she offers the book but never forces it.
Encouragement 2	2	The mother offers the toy and later the book.
Encouragement 3	2	The mother moves the toy to help the child and says okay when the child first says no to reading the book.
Encouragement 4	2	The mother suggests that the child read the animals a book.
Encouragement 5	2	The mother offers verbal encouragement throughout, particularly when she suggests the book.
Encouragement 6	0	The mother offers no suggestions to help the child with what she is already doing.
Encouragement 7	2	The mother pays attention, talks, and helps throughout.
Teaching 1	2	The mother says, "Lee el libro para que se duerman" [Read the book to fall asleep]. She gives the reason for reading a book.
Teaching 2	2	The mother suggests that the child read the animals a book.
Teaching 3	2	The mother repeats the child's words throughout. She says, "Todos se durmieron" [Everyone slept].
Teaching 4	1	The mother labels "libro" [book] and "los animales" [the animals]. She does not make a direct connection, just says the names in context.
Teaching 5	1	The mother holds/moves the house. She verbally pretends but does not engage more than once or twice.
Teaching 6	0	The mother follows no direct sequence of steps.
Teaching 7	0	The mother never uses adjectives when talking about objects.
Teaching 8	1	The mother says, "¿Y a qué vamos a hacer?" [And what will we do?], asking the child what they are going to do, but this seems like a rhetorical question because the mother then goes on to say, "¡Ya sé!" [I know!] and explains a plan to read to the animals.

FIVE-MINUTE OBSERVATION: SPANISH

Item	Code	Rationale
Affection 1	2	The mother speaks in a warm, inviting tone throughout.
Affection 2	2	The mother smiles at the child several times.
Affection 3	0	The mother never directly praises the child.
Affection 4	2	The mother is consistently within arm's reach and leans toward the child.
Affection 5	0	The mother never uses nicknames or other positive expressions.
Affection 6	2	The mother engages with the child consistently throughout. She plays with the toys but is always clearly focused on the child and helps the child play with the toys.
Affection 7	2	The mother smiles and laughs consistently. It is clear she is interested and enjoying herself.
Responsiveness 1	2	The mother comments on the child's actions consistently throughout and shows interest.
Responsiveness 2	2	The mother tries a new activity (new idea with the same activity).
Responsiveness 3	2	The mother allows the child to grab and play with the toys.
Responsiveness 4	2	As described previously, the mother never forces or makes the child do anything. She makes suggestions and leads the playing at times.
Responsiveness 5	2	The mother responds to the child's positive emotions. She laughs, smiles, and plays.
Responsiveness 6	2	The mother looks at the child consistently, several times.

Item	Code	Rationale
Responsiveness 7	2	The mother says, "¿Sí? OK" [Yeah? Okay] "¿Allí? OK" [There? Okay], "Oy. ¡Ya sé!" [Oh, I know], "¿Todos despertaron?" [They are all waking up?], and "¿Quién quiere morado?" [Who wants the purple one?].
Encouragement 1	2	After making suggestions, the mother allows the child to do the activity. She does not do it for her.
Encouragement 2	2	The mother points out objects, but allows the child to play with the toys herself.
Encouragement 3	2	The mother suggests that the rings could be food and helps the child play with them.
Encouragement 4	2	The mother constantly supports the child to do her own thing. Examples are when she suggests the mats could be beds for the animals. She lets the child put the animals there. She also allows the child to be the one to "feed" the animals.
Encouragement 5	2	The mother verbally encourages the child constantly throughout. She has a back-and-forth play commentary encouraging the child's play.
Encouragement 6	0	The mother never suggests something for the express purpose of helping the child with the activity at hand.
Encouragement 7	2	The mother is very engaged, laughs and smiles, and is involved.
Teaching 1	1	The mother says, "Ya todos mis animales están dormidos. Así que ya no hables que fuerte" [My animals are all asleep, so don't talk loud].
Teaching 2	2	The mother suggests activities throughout. She suggests feeding animals to extend the play with them.
Teaching 3	2	The mother repeats the child's words throughout: "Allí" [There], "¡Sí!" [Yes], "¿Todos despertaron?" [They all woke up?], "¿Quién quiere?" [Who wants it?], and so forth.
Teaching 4	2	The mother labels *beds, house, food,* and *animals.*
Teaching 5	2	The mother engages in pretend play during the entire video clip.
Teaching 6	0	At no point does the mother do a specific sequence of steps or talk about something that shows a clear order.
Teaching 7	2	The mother talks about the colors of the rings, the animals being hungry, loud and soft voices, and so forth.
Teaching 8	2	The mother asks, "¿Qué hacemos?" [What should we do?] and "¿Cuál le falta de comer?" [Which one hasn't eaten yet?].

TEN-MINUTE OBSERVATION: SPANISH

Item	Code	Rationale
Affection 1	2	The mother is consistently warm throughout.
Affection 2	2	The mother smiles at the child consistently throughout.
Affection 3	0	The mother never says something directly praising the child or what she is doing.
Affection 4	2	The mother is always within arm's reach and is consistently leaning in toward the child.
Affection 5	0	The mother never uses an affectionate nickname or positive expression.
Affection 6	2	The mother interacts with the child constantly throughout the video clip.
Affection 7	2	The mother shows enjoyment and positive emotion throughout the video clip.
Responsiveness 1	2	The mother is very involved in the child's activity. She talks to her, plays with her, and so forth.

Item	Code	Rationale
Responsiveness 2	2	The mother is focused on the child's needs throughout. She puts down the book but makes sure the child is done with the book before moving on.
Responsiveness 3	2	The child is quite engaged throughout, but the mother allows the child to switch toys or activities whenever she wants.
Responsiveness 4	2	The mother offers new suggestions but never forces the child to change activities, as described previously.
Responsiveness 5	2	The child only shows positive emotions, but the mother smiles and laughs along with the child.
Responsiveness 6	2	The mother looks at the child multiple times when the child speaks, laughs, or vocalizes.
Responsiveness 7	2	The mother replies to the child multiple times. She says, "¿Te siente mal?" [It feels bad?], "¿Es una casa?" [It's a house?], "¿Es un barquito?" [A little boat?], "¿Es un hipo?" [It's a hippo?], and "Oh, ¿No quieres cantar?" [Oh, you don't want to sing?].
Encouragement 1	2	During the switch from the book to toys, the mother suggests the change then waits to get confirmation from the child.
Encouragement 2	2	The mother encourages the child to touch the book, puts new toys in the child's lap to play with, and pulls the toys closer to the child.
Encouragement 3	2	The mother never forces the child to do anything. She makes lots of suggestions but ultimately allows the child to choose what she is doing throughout the video clip.
Encouragement 4	2	The mother plays alongside the child throughout the video clip. She does not take anything from her. She allows the child to play with toys in her own way.
Encouragement 5	2	The mother talks to the child constantly throughout the video clip about the toys, the activities, and what the child is doing. She makes suggestions of things the child could do.
Encouragement 6	1	Several times, the mother suggests things the child could do to extend the activity or to keep going. The child does not struggle much though, so the mother does not help a lot.
Encouragement 7	2	The mother shows enthusiasm consistently throughout. She is very enthusiastic about the activities and playing with the child.
Teaching 1	2	The mother says, "¿Los pongamos en la escalera? Eso para que bajen por la escalera" [Let's put them on the stairs. So they can go down the stairs], "Agarrar lo para que camine. Camina despacito, por que no se despiertan" [Grab it so we can walk. Walk slowly so they don't wake up], and "Shhh, se van a dormir" [Quiet because they're going to sleep].
Teaching 2	2	The mother suggests activities constantly. She suggests putting the animals to sleep and feeling the book, among others.
Teaching 3	2	The mother repeats, "¿un banquito?" [a stool?] "¿Cuántos muchachos hay?" [How many boys are there?], and "Dos. Dos." [Two. Two.]
Teaching 4	2	The mother labels "jirafa" [giraffe], "elephante" [elephant], "barco" [boat], "perro" [dog], and "rasposo" [scraping], among others.
Teaching 5	2	The mother engages in pretend play with the toy animals for most of the video clip.
Teaching 6	1	The mother says, "¿Los pongamos en la escalera? Eso para que bajen por la escalera." [Let's put them on the stairs. So they can go down the stairs], but this is very subtle as a sequence and more of a suggestion and explanation.
Teaching 7	2	The mother says, "grande jirafa" [big giraffe] and "¿Qué dice el hipo?" [What does the hippo say?]. She makes elephant noises and gives the quantities of objects.
Teaching 8	2	The mother asks, "¿Cuántos muchachos hay?" [How many boys are there?] and "¿De qué color es la jirafa?" [What color is the giraffe?].

Index

Page numbers followed by *f* indicate figures; those followed by *t* indicate tables.